The Other Twelve

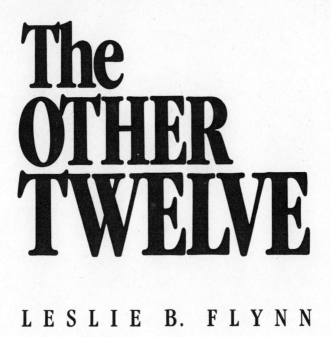

The OTHER TWELVE

LESLIE B. FLYNN

While this book is intended for the reader's personal enjoyment and profit, it is also intended for group study. A Leader's Guide with Victor Multiuse Transparency Masters is available from your local bookstore or from the publisher.

VICTOR BOOKS®

A DIVISION OF SCRIPTURE PRESS PUBLICATIONS INC.
USA CANADA ENGLAND

Unless otherwise noted, Scripture quotations are from the King James Version. Quotations marked NIV are from the *Holy Bible, New International Version,* © 1973, 1978, 1984, International Bible Society. Used by permission of Zondervan Bible Publishers. Quotations marked NASB are from the *New American Standard Bible,* © the Lockman Foundation 1960, 1962, 1963, 1968, 1971, 1972, 1973, 1975, 1977. Quotations marked PH are from J.B. Phillips: *The New Testament in Modern English,* Revised Edition, © J.B. Phillips, 1958, 1960, 1972, permission of Macmillan Publishing Co. and Collins Publishers.

Recommended Dewey Decimal Classification: 225.92

Suggested Subject Heading: Bible-Biography

Library of Congress Catalog Card Number: 88-060213

ISBN: 0-89693-423-3

CONTENTS

DEDICATION

To Edison and Kay,
Harry and Peggy,
friends of 40 years,
our extended family.

INTRODUCTION

The Twelve is the highly honored titled given those intimate followers of Jesus whom He called, trained, and commissioned to preach the Gospel to all nations. Not quite as well known as the Twelve Apostles is another group of twelve who, during the same time period, worked valiantly to spread the Good News throughout the Roman Empire.

Whereas the Twelve Apostles gathered around the Lord Jesus, this second group of twelve associated with the Apostle Paul. Except Stephen who knew Paul only as Saul, a relentless persecutor, each of the twelve became Paul's friends after his conversion. Although Stephen did not know Paul as a friend, it was his magnificent martyrdom that played a major part in Paul's conversion. Today in heaven Paul and Stephen are doubtless the best of friends.

Paul had a wide circle of friends, some of whom may seem, in the judgment of others, more deserving of a spot on this roster of *The Other Twelve.* But we have selected for discussion those characters who seem most prominent in New Testament history. Perhaps a more discreet title would have been *Another Twelve.*

Just as Jesus had the traitor Judas among His followers, so Paul had the defector Demas among his companions. We have included a chapter on Demas.

These chapters present the characters in the chronological order in which they entered Paul's life.

1. Stephen, the Martyr

A wealthy Oriental man took his little daughter to a missionary school, willing to pay any expense. The father, however, didn't want his daughter to enroll as a student, but merely to remain only long enough for the missionaries to put something on her face to make her as beautiful as the other girls at the school. The missionary in charge of the school explained that nothing was put on the girls' faces to make them pretty.

"Then why are they better-looking than the girls in our towns? When girls come here they are just plain-looking, but before long they become pretty. What do you put on their faces?"

The missionary replied, "It's not something we put on their faces, but Someone they receive into their hearts."

When Stephen faced the Sanhedrin to defend the Gospel, all the members of the council "saw that his face was like the face of an angel" (Acts 6:15, NIV). Filled with the Spirit, he radiated the glory of Christ. An enthusiastic, energetic, effervescent man, Stephen was full of wisdom, full of faith, full of God's grace, and full of God's power (6:3, 5, 8 NIV), a well-rounded saint indeed.

The story of Stephen covers only two chapters (Acts 6 and 7), with an additional reference to him as a martyr by Paul in Acts 22:20. So dynamic was he with his unanswerable wisdom, persuasive eloquence, and overflowing zeal, that he was the first believer to be martyred. We can sum up his life by describing his four roles: deacon, apologist, martyr, and victor.

Deacon

Often we lament, "If only we could return to the good old days of the apostolic church." Recalling how the believers at Jerusalem faithfully practiced doctrine, fellowship, communion, and prayer, we create a fantasy of perfection, a church without problems. The church was increasing numerically, thriving in the wake of Pentecost. The record reads, "The multitude of them that believed were of one heart and soul: neither said any of them that ought of the things which he possessed was his own; but they had all things common" (Acts 4:32).

But a growing membership doesn't guarantee harmony. Here, success created a tense situation. The very demonstration of love shown in the sharing of resources by the wealthy to alleviate the poverty of the less fortunate was the point at which Satan tried to gain a foothold in this ideal community. The Grecian Jews complained that their widows were being overlooked in the daily distribution of charity by the Hebrews in the community. Though some prejudice may have been present, most likely the neglect was accidental. As the numbers grew, the task of distribution simply required more supervision than the apostles could give.

Since the peace of the church was in jeopardy, action had

to be taken. The apostles did not ignore the complaint but proposed a plan to deal with it. Not wishing to be diverted from their priorities of prayer and ministry of the Word, they said, "Select from among you, brethren, seven men . . . whom we may put in charge of this task" (Acts 6:3, NASB). The seven were to be of good reputation and full of the Holy Spirit and wisdom. Interestingly, the humble duties of table serving called for sterling Christian graces as well as sanctified common sense, enabling the servers to administer tactfully and lovingly in the delicate situation.

Significantly, those chosen all bear Greek names as though the Hebrews said in a generous act of peacemaking, "You think your widows are being neglected; then choose Grecian men to distribute the food. We're trusting the entire operation to you."

Stephen's name appears first on the list. His outstanding character had already gained him recognition as a leader. With Spirit-given wisdom he was able to lead the other six to handle the affair so that no split occurred in the ranks. In fact, the Word of God spread, numbers increased rapidly, and a large group of priests accepted Christ (Acts 6:7).

In 1 Timothy 3:8-13 Paul gives the qualifications for the office of deacon as we know it. In many churches today deacons are responsible for the church's charitable work, among other duties. Some Bible scholars regard Stephen and the other six men chosen to assume the charitable duties of the early church as the first deacons even though the title, *deacon,* is not used in the Acts 6 account.

Just before the battle of Trafalgar in 1805 the British naval commander Lord Nelson learned that a captain and an admiral were at odds. He sent for the two men. Placing the right hands of the two men together, Lord Nelson said, pointing to the opposing navy, "Look—over there is the enemy!"

Stephen was also able to unite the two potential factions

to face the common enemy who would soon break upon them with great fury. Like Stephen, we are called to be peacemakers so that the members of our fellowship may live together in unity.

Apologist

Stephen's speech is the first apologetic sermon on record. Peter's Pentecost sermon was more evangelistic, though it did contain some element of apologetics. The term *apologetics* comes from the Greek word *apologia* which means a speech in defense. Apologetics then, is a theological discipline devoted to the defense of the divine origin and authority of Christianity. Peter told us always to be ready to give an answer (apologia) to everyone asking a reason for the hope within us (1 Peter 3:15).

In the first few centuries apologists (those who speak or write in defense of a faith, a cause, or an institution) defended the church against accusations of atheism, immorality, and treason. Later in the Middle Ages apologists had to turn their attention to adversaries and heresies within the church. In the eighteenth century, they faced the issues of naturalism and deism.

Today, every evangelical seminary offers courses on apologetics. Works of more recent popular apologists include: *Know What You Believe* and *Know Why You Believe* by Paul Little; *Evidence that Demands a Verdict* by Josh McDowell; *Mere Christianity* by C.S. Lewis; and many books by Francis Schaeffer.

In the days of the early church, Stephen, as a serious student of the Old Testament, a powerful reasoner, and persuasive communicator so capably defended the faith that leaders in the various synagogues of Jerusalem could not resist the wisdom and spirit by which he spoke (6:9-10). In retaliation for their humiliating inability to refute Stephen's arguments, the elders stirred up the people against Stephen, set up false witnesses, arrested him, and brought him before the Sanhedrin.

The charges against him included blasphemy against Moses and against God. The Sanhedrin claimed he said that Jesus of Nazareth would destroy their temple and change Moses' customs. As the charges were made, everyone saw something remarkable. Stephen's face shone like an angel's. Did some of them recall how Moses' face shone in Old Testament times? Stephen seems to have had more in common with Moses than did his accusers.

When Stephen's murderers saw in his face something that looked like an angel, it was only the reflection of what was in his heart. With its 80 muscles that can create more than 7,000 expressions, the face has been called "the mirror of the soul." In Charles Dickens' *Tale of Two Cities* Sidney Carton voluntarily went to the guillotine, taking the place of another man. It was said that night that "his was the peacefullest man's face ever beheld at the guillotine."

Robert Murray McCheyne, Scottish pastor, left an indelible mark through his sermons though he died at the early age of 30. One congregant said, "His holiness was noticeable even before he spoke a word. His appearance spoke for him" ("Beloved Minister," *Faith for the Family,* February 1986, p. 6).

The main arguments of Stephen's defense may be summed up under two points. First, Stephen explained that God's revelation to Israel was never bound to one place like the temple, nor to one person like Moses. Long before the temple and Moses, the Lord dealt with Abraham in Chaldea, and Joseph in Egypt. That the revelation was progressive, gradual, and incomplete in Moses was shown by Moses' own prediction. "A prophet shall God raise up unto you from among your brethren, like unto me" (Acts 7:37).

The *second* strand of Stephen's defense is the repeated resistance of Israel to God's new revelations. The fathers of the nation had turned away from Moses at the very moment he was receiving the Ten Commandments. Instead of obeying the divine instructions, the nation turned to idolatry. Whenever the prophets warned the Israelites of their dead ritualism and need of repentance, they persecuted the seers, killing many. Their disposition to disobey the divine revelation persisted till its awful culmination in the betrayal and murder of the Righteous One (Acts 7:52). Though Stephen never mentioned the name of Jesus in his address, his hearers could not help but catch the parallels with Joseph and Moses, both types of Christ, who were first mistreated but later rose to rulership. The Jesus they now repulsed would be raised as Lord, Stephen implied. He also implied that God's program called for a universal Gospel offer, which ran counter to their narrow Judaism.

Stephen boldly and directly accused his accusers of resisting the Holy Spirit and killing the Sinless One. These charges angered his audience as did his irrefutable arguments based on their own Scripture. They stopped his speech.

Martyr

Stephen's sermon so enraged the members of the Sanhedrin that they began gnashing their teeth at him. Stephen, filled with the Holy Spirit, looked heavenward, saw the glory of God, and announced what he saw. He said, "I see the heavens opened up and the Son of man standing at the right hand of God" (Acts 7:56, NASB). Then the council members cried out with a loud voice, plugged their ears, and attacked him. Casting him out of the city, they stoned him (7:57-58, NASB).

The practice of stoning first occurred in the deserts of stony Arabia where an abundance of rocks likely suggested this mode of execution. Originally, the citizens merely pelted their victim, but specific protocol gradually developed. A crier paraded before the accused man, heralding his offense. The victim was usually placed on something high, then thrown down from this height before he was crushed with the stones hurled at him. Stoning was the mode of capital punishment usual for the crimes of blasphemy and idolatry (Deut. 13:9-10; 17:5-7). Those who had brought witness against the victim were required to cast the first stones. To give themselves freedom of movement for forceful throwing, the witnesses against Stephen removed their outer garments and laid them at the feet of Saul for safeguarding, never dreaming of the tremendous impact Stephen's behavior in martyrdom would have on this ringleader-zealot.

This was nothing but a common lynching. The members of the Sanhedrin in their fury didn't take time for a vote, nor did they bother to consult the Romans. They could claim the event an uprising of the people, and thus justify Stephen's death.

Similarities to Christ's death. Stephen's death is the only one in the New Testament apart from Christ's which is related with any degree of detail. Scripture tells us that James was beheaded, but John, Peter, Paul, and John all pass from the pages of Scripture without mention of their deaths. The death of Stephen, however, is recorded in an unforgettable manner. Perhaps the reason such attention is given to the way Stephen died is the similarity to the way Jesus died. Some parallels include:

- Both were accused by false witnesses of blaspheming the temple.
- Both prayed for their persecutors. The first cry from the cross was the prayer for forgiveness, "Father, forgive them; for they know not what they do" (Luke

23:34). As Stephen's body, battered by stones, slowly disintegrated into a mass of bruised and bleeding pulp, he went to his knees and cried with a loud voice, "Lord, lay not this sin to their charge" (Acts 7:60).

- Both offered a prayer of commitment to the Lord. Jesus, with a loud voice, said, "Father, into Thy hands I commend My spirit" (Luke 23:46). Stephen prayed, "Lord Jesus, receive my spirit" (Acts 7:59).
- Both were buried by sympathetic men. Nicodemus and Joseph of Arimathea, secret believers, came into the open at a very hostile moment to give Jesus an honorable burial in a private, unused tomb (John 19:38-39). Several followers of Stephen treated him in a similar way: "Devout men carried Stephen to his burial, and made great lamentation over him" (Acts 8:2).
- Both went to the Father. Forty days after His death, Jesus ascended to His Father. Stephen went immediately into the presence of Christ who ushered the martyr into the presence of the Father at whose right hand Stephen had seen Jesus standing.

Since Stephen was so under the control of the Spirit, whose mission is to produce Christ's likeness in us, it's not surprising that Stephen resembled Christ, even in death.

Similarities to other martyrs. Stephen was first in the list of deacons, first in the line of apologists, and first in the long line of martyrs. Untold myriads have since died for the faith. *Foxe's Book of Martyrs* contains nearly 500 pages of the history of those who forfeited their lives instead of renouncing their Saviour. The book contains detailed accounts of unbelievable methods of torture and death, beginning with the time of the disciples and continuing to the sixteenth century.

Polycarp, Bishop of Smyrna and disciple of John, is one of

the best known of the early martyrs. Those who apprehended him were amazed at his serene countenance much like the crowd was amazed at Stephen's countenance. After serving his captors a meal, he asked for an hour to pray. With permission granted he prayed with such fervency that some of the guards were sorry they had captured him. He was taken before the proconsul, however, where he was asked to swear by Caesar and thus deny Christ. Polycarp answered, "Fourscore and six years have I been His servant, and He hath done me no wrong. How then can I blaspheme my King who saved me?"

When this was proclaimed to the whole multitude in the stadium, several in the crowd cried out loudly and with ungovernable wrath, "This is the teacher of Asia, the father of the Christians, the puller down of our gods, who teacheth numbers not to sacrifice nor worship." They shouted to the proconsul to let a lion loose on Polycarp, but the proconsul replied that it was not lawful since he had brought the sport to a close. Then in unison the crowd shouted that Polycarp should be burnt alive.

Timber and faggots were gathered from workshops and baths. When the pile was ready and they were about to nail him to the stake, he said, "Leave me as I am; for He that hath granted me to endure the fire will grant me also to remain at the pile unmoved, even without the security which ye seek from the nails." So they did not nail him, but tied him. Then he prayed. "I bless Thee for that Thou hast granted me this day and hour, that I might receive a portion amongst the number of martyrs. . . . May I be received among these in Thy presence this day, as a rich and acceptable sacrifice. . . . For this cause, yea and for all things, I praise Thee, I bless Thee, I glorify Thee, through the eternal and heavenly High Priest, Jesus Christ, Thy beloved Son."

The fire was lit. Though the heat became intolerable to

the executioners, the accounts of Polycarp's martyrdom report that he sang hymns in the midst of the flames, somehow remaining untouched by them. His executioners speared him to death and burnt his corpse.

In the twentieth century more Christians have been martyred than in all previous centuries of church history. Countless people have perished under the Communist regime in China. The best-known victims were probably John and Betty Stam who were slain in 1934. Thousands of national believers, as well as many missionaries, died because of persecutions in Colombia, South America, in the '50s. Who has not heard of the five brave young American missionaries killed by the Aucas deep in the Ecuadorian jungle in 1956? Later, dozens of missionaries paid the supreme sacrifice in the Congo (now Zaire) in the '60s. In the '70s Christian and Missionary Alliance missionaries were murdered in Vietnam.

In January 1981 Chet Bitterman, a Wycliffe missionary about to begin language study in Colombia, was kidnapped by six terrorists. After 48 days of captivity, filled with threats, deadlines, and rumors, the missionary was shot by rebels who left his body in a hijacked bus.

In the long annals of the Christian church nothing is more moving than the boldness and fearlessness with which the saints have faced persecution. Like their forerunner Stephen, they have been ready to face stoning, fire, or the "lion's gory mane" in the arena. Most Christians will not be called on to pay this supreme sacrifice. The Bible, however, teaches that all who live righteously will suffer persecution (2 Tim. 3:12). Sometimes living for Christ may be more difficult than dying for Him. Perhaps the gift of martyrdom which 1 Corinthians 13:3 hints at when it says, "though I give my body to be burned," is the spirit of willingness to suffer persecution even to the point of death.

Victor

As a result of Stephen's death, members of the early church suffered a severe blow. How could God do this to them? They had lost their champion defender of the faith. Who would or could take his place? Before long they discovered that God can transform tragedy into triumph and make the wrath of men to praise Him. To the persecuted church at Smyrna mentioned in Revelation and to all martyrs comes the promise, "Be thou faithful unto death, and I will give thee a crown of life" (Rev. 2:10). Salvation is a gift, but crowns are earned. How appropriate that Stephen's name means crown.

Stephen emboldened others to stand up for Jesus. Those who buried Stephen did so at the risk of their own lives. Just as at a mobster's funeral, police survey the mourners to see who his friends might be, so the persecutors would watch to see who claimed Stephen's body.

Undeterred by the danger and motivated by his courageous example, "devout men carried Stephen to his burial, and made great lamentation over him" (Acts 8:2).

Stephen's death also affected Paul. Though other factors played a part in Paul's conversion, Stephen's magnificent martyrdom kept goading Saul until he finally capitulated on the Damascus road. Loaded with antichristian hate, Saul had set out to ravage the church in distant places. So energetic was his zeal that he had secured official papers to jail people 100 miles away in Damascus, yet Saul found it hard to kick against the pricks of conscience and memory. Stephen's angelic face, committal of his spirit to the waiting Lord, and forgiveness of his enemies, led to a sudden turnabout in the life of Saul. Confronted by the risen Christ, persecutor Saul became preacher Paul.

Stephen was a victor after all. When Paul was martyred, doubtless no one gave him a warmer welcome to heaven than Stephen who could justifiably claim Paul as his trophy, joy, and crown.

The mantle of Stephen fell on Paul. Stephen was the prototype for Paul. The dictionary defines prototype as "an original model on which something is patterned." What Stephen was, Paul became. Preaching the same universal message and mission of Christianity as Stephen's sermon suggested, Paul ministered as the apostle to the Gentiles. Often, like Stephen, he faced the same venom of Judaizers' opposition to his offer of free salvation to both Gentile and Jew. Paul, like his prototype, was a master apologist and defender of the faith.

Dr. C. Everett Koop, Surgeon General, United States Public Health Service, writes of a situation which, like Stephen's death, seemed to be a tragedy but became a victory. He writes that his world turned upside down when his 20-year-old son, David, died in a mountain climbing accident. He says, "When news of his death came, I can't describe the absolute desolation I felt. But fifteen minutes after I heard the news I gathered my family together, put my arms around as many of them as I could, and prayed, 'Heavenly Father, we know that David is Your son and that You gave him to us for a while. Now You've seen fit to take him back. We don't understand this. Please show us something that You will accomplish by putting us through this.' "

Refusing to cancel a speaking engagement at a large church near Philadelphia the Sunday after David's death, Dr Koop spoke about heart transplants and how God can give us new spiritual hearts. In the middle of the message he suddenly stopped and said, "Now that's as far as I have prepared because something terrible happened in my life last week." Then he told them about David's death and his conviction that God was in charge and had a purpose in the tragedy.

Unknown to Dr. Koop a friend taped that message and printed it as a tract with a picture of a transplanted heart. That tract had a widespread ministry with more than 8 million copies printed in several languages. People told him, "My life was turned around by your tract on transplanted hearts." Dr. Koop feels this is one way David accomplished much for the cause of Christ by his death.

After David's death, Koop hung in his office a picture of his son in hiking clothes, standing on a New Hampshire mountain. So striking was the picture that few people ever left the office without asking, "Is that your son?" He would reply, "Yes. Shortly after that picture was taken, he was killed while climbing." Dr. Koop would then tell them of his grief but also of his faith in the sovereignty of God. He would say, "David was taken from us for reasons we may never know, but I can give you a long list of what we do know now." At that time Koop was surgeon-in-chief of The Children's Hospital in Philadelphia, Pennsylvania. He would say to parents in his office, "If I were not completely convinced of the sovereignty of God, I couldn't take care of your child." He said the effect was amazing ("God's Plan for a Surgeon," *Decision,* Dec. 1985).

The death of Stephen was, at first, an inexplicable mystery to the early church. But from the perspective of a few decades later, the calamity proved to be a major event in God's great sovereign plan for the advancement of His church.

2. Barnabas, the Supporter

For years my wife has followed a set of six daily rules which she adopted from an anonymous source. She resolves every day to do something for herself, to do something she doesn't want to do but which needs doing, to do a physical exercise, to do a mental exercise, and to offer an original prayer that includes thanks for blessings. The sixth item (though first on her list) is to do something for someone else. Since she does this without telling anyone, including me, I cannot give many examples, though I have discovered her taking food to a shut-in.

This attitude of helping others is especially obvious in one New Testament character. His name is Barnabas. But that is not his real name. As I now mention his original name, you probably do not recognize him because Joses helped people so much that he was given a new name by the apostles. According to Acts 4:36, the apostles called him Barnabas, which means "the son of consolation." Other versions translate his name, "son of encouragement," "son of comfort," and "son of exhortation."

Though we know little of his intellectual brilliance, we know him to be a man of warm heart and open hand. He moves through the narrative of Acts like John Bunyan's Great-heart moves through the story *Pilgrim's Progress,* always disposed to kindness, consideration, and sympathy. Some would rank Barnabas next to Paul, among New Testament luminaries; others would place him among the lesser lights, perhaps because he left us no authentic writing and also because he drops from view after his altercation with Paul. Actually, Barnabas deserves a spot among the stars of first magnitude, a little below Paul, John, and Peter, but on a level with James, the brother of Jesus.

The apostles and disciples had seen Barnabas encourage and comfort so many people that his real name faded from use. He was known everywhere in the church as the comforter and the exhorter. In fact, every time Barnabas appears in the sacred record he is encouraging someone.

He Helped Feed the Hungry
Tradition places Barnabas among the 70 sent out by Jesus, and 1 of the 500 brethren who saw the risen Christ. But the New Testament gives no hint of Barnabas as a disciple before Pentecost. A Greek-speaking Jew from a family who had settled on the island of Cyprus, he may well have been present in Jerusalem on the Day of Pentecost, becoming a Christian through Peter's sermon that day or through the flood tide of fervor which followed that occasion. Whether or not he returned to Cyprus to witness to his family and friends, we are not told. Likely, he remained in Jerusalem where he became a leading figure.

The first church contained many poor people. Confession of Christ made it difficult to secure or hold a job. In addition to these poor people, some of the pilgrims from other nations who were converted on the day of Pentecost probably remained in Jerusalem for instruction and fellowship, thus swelling the need for financial resources. Local believers had to help. When well-to-do believers decided to sell property or houses to create a common fund from which the apostles would relieve needs, landowner Barnabas did not hesitate to sell his land, probably on his native island of Cyprus, and bring the full amount of the proceeds to the treasury of the church to alleviate temporal needs. The favorable reaction of the church to this act of complete renunciation probably aroused the envy of Ananias and Sapphira who sold their property and pretended to bring the entire profit to the church. They lost their lives because of their deception.

Our first picture of Barnabas, then, is that of a man of generous action toward the common people, despite his seeming aristocratic background. After selling his property, Barnabas may even have had to toil at some trade to make a living. Paul hints at this in 1 Corinthians 9:6.

Barnabas was involved in feeding the hungry on a second occasion. Under the rule of the Roman Emperor Claudius (A.D. 41-54) the land around the Mediterranean suffered several famines due to the failure of corn crops. The prediction of widespread famine by the prophet Agabus aroused pity in the church at Antioch where Barnabas was the top leader. The church members knew how severe the suffering would be in the Holy City and surrounding area, so the church at Antioch, every member according to his ability, decided to provide help for their brothers in Judea. This assistance was sent to the Jerusalem elders "by the hands of Barnabas and Saul" (Acts 11:30).

Even the most casual reading of the Bible reminds us of God's concern for the hungry. The law of gleaning forbad the farmer who missed a sheaf to go back and get it, or to glean the olive bough a second time. Grapes missed the first time were to be left on the vine (Lev. 19:9-10). This permission to glean would keep the poor from going hungry.

We also read in Scripture that divine blessing rests on those who feed the hungry: "If you spend yourselves on behalf of the hungry and satisfy the needs of the oppressed, then your light will rise in darkness, and your night will become like the noonday" (Isa. 58:10, NIV). Proverbs teaches that the one who pities the poor lends to the Lord and will be repaid whatever he gives. Proverbs also teaches that the one who shuts his ear to the cry of the poor will find himself crying out unheard (19:17; 21:13). The New Testament contains this theme of feeding the hungry, warning that those who fail to help a hungry brother possess a spurious faith and empty love (James 2:15-17; 1 John 3:17). Jesus set an example for us by feeding the hungry on more than one occasion.

Pulse, The Evangelical Missions Information Service (July 3, 1986), says that Mother Teresa, known for her self-denying ministry among the unfortunates of India, has feet twisted with arthritis, possesses sight in only one eye, and sleeps only three hours a night. She spends time with every visitor to her Calcutta headquarters. Though we may not be called to demonstrate that degree of dedication, every believer should examine his conscience and his actions to make sure that he is practicing concrete compassion to the deprived and destitute in his own country and in needy parts of the world. Though pictures and reports of sub–Sahara hunger may overwhelm us, they should not blind us to the fact that, though by ourselves we cannot solve the problem of Africa's starving people, every one of us can and must do something. For example, we can give according to our ability through responsible organizations like World Relief, the official relief arm of the National Association of Evangelicals. The money we send will be channeled through our evangelical counterparts on the mission field to reach the needy.

Like Barnabas, we must be willing to help the poor and the hungry. Significantly, the Greek word for *consolation* found in Barnabas' name, contains the same Greek root as the title Paraclete, given to the Holy Spirit. The title simply means, "one called alongside to help." Indeed, Barnabas did come alongside to help the poor and the hungry in Jerusalem.

He Vouched for a Questionable Convert

Picture Paul's predicament as he headed back to Jerusalem after his conversion. He knew he would be rejected, even persecuted by the Sanhedrin, to whom his conversion came as shocking news. His old friends considered him a traitor.

No one could forget about the Christians whom he had so violently mistreated. He had thrown men and women into prison. He had held the garments of those who stoned Stephen. The last his friends heard of him, he was on his way to Damascus, breathing out threats of murder against believers in Damascus. He was armed with official letters from the high priest instructing him to arrest, bind, and bring back to Jerusalem any followers of Christ, whether men or women. For one who had so attacked the church to suddenly become a zealous follower of Christ seemed incredible. Had it not happened so far away from Jerusalem, it might have seemed more believable.

When Paul arrived back in Jerusalem after his conversion, he "was trying to associate with the disciples; and they were all afraid of him" (Acts 9:26 NASB). The tense of the verbs indicates Paul's repeated attempts to win their acceptance. The disciples simply did not believe Paul's conversion was genuine. Might this just be a ruse to obtain the names of more believers to be arrested and slain?

The situation was crucial. Paul wished to be accepted by the church's leaders, but they shrank from him lest he turn out to be an infiltrator. If he were rejected, the leaders wondered, would Paul be lost to the cause of Christ? Or would he develop his own following?

Now Barnabas enters the situation. Taking Paul, literally, by the hand, Barnabas "brought him to the apostles, and declared unto them how [Paul] had seen the Lord in the way, and that He had spoken to him, and how [Paul] had preached boldly at Damascus in the name of Jesus" (Acts 9:27). Basically, Barnabas argued, "You must give Paul a chance. I'm convinced of his sincerity." Risking his reputation, Barnabas sponsored Paul's cause so well that the questionable convert "was with them coming in and going out at Jerusalem" (Acts 9:28). Barnabas was the first man of stature at headquarters who opened his heart to Saul of Tarsus when all Jerusalem was still suspicious of him.

Suspicion also surrounded Chuck Colson's conversion. People could not believe that Nixon's hatchet man had really changed. *What trick is he up to now?* people thought. Not long after his profession of faith, Colson was invited to an early morning prayer meeting in the basement of the White House west wing. At this biweekly meeting some government leaders shared their faith, read Scriptures, and prayed together. Harold Hughes, who had only once been invited to the White House during Nixon's term, was invited by the group to one of their meetings. Hughes, in turn, invited Colson. On arrival Colson noticed men who had not been his buddies, including one on whom he had played a dirty trick a few years before. Asked to say a few words, Hughes spoke for twenty minutes with devastating honesty about how Christ had changed his life, conflicts he faced as a Christian in government, and then how he had come to know his brother in Christ, Chuck Colson.

Colson comments, "If it had not been such a moving moment, I would have laughed aloud at the astonished expressions around the room."

"Hughes continued, 'I've learned how wrong it is to hate. For years there were men towards whom I felt consuming bitterness. By hating I was shutting Christ's love out of my life. One of the men I hated most was Chuck Colson, but now that we share a commitment together in Christ, I love him as my brother. I would trust him with my life, my family, with everything I have.' "

When he finished there was a long silence. The man on whom Colson had played that dirty trick was to close the meeting. He cleared his throat. It was plain that he was choking back tears. After mumbling a thanks to Harold Hughes, he took Colson's right hand in his left and said, "Now I would like to ask Mr. Colson to lead us in prayer." Everyone joined hands. As Colson ended his prayer in which he expressed the need for all to depend on God's wisdom and power to direct the affairs of the nation, he felt the hand of the man he had tricked tighten its grip. Says Colson, "Many clasped me by the arm, welcoming me to a fraternal bond much closer than what we knew as White House staff" (Chuck Colson, *Born Again,* Spire Books, p. 162). Because of Harold Hughes, Colson was welcomed as a new believer in Christ. Because of Barnabas, Paul was welcomed as a new believer in Christ.

He Welcomed Gentile Believers
Not only did Barnabas endorse an unwelcome convert, but he also accepted some irregular saints.

Believers from the early church, scattered by persecution, went everywhere preaching the Gospel. Most believers preached to Jews; however, some shared the Gospel with Gentiles in Antioch, the capital of Syria, center of vast trade, and famous for the learning of its citizens. Antioch was located at the very summit of its glory and known as the third city of the Roman Empire. The Lord blessed this witness in Antioch; a large number of Gentiles believed in Christ. To the leaders at Jerusalem, the result was a seemingly alien church, so they commissioned Barnabas as a committee of one to investigate the church.

The Jerusalem church should not have thought the situation so unusual because Philip had started a church of despised half-Jewish Samaritans, on which both Peter and John had placed their stamp of approval (Acts 8:5-17). Also, Peter had preached the Gospel to Cornelius' Gentile household in Caesarea, which matter the Jerusalem church had tacitly sanctioned just before word came of the Antioch episode (Acts 11:1-18).

The choice of Barnabas to investigate the church in Antioch indicates the high esteem with which he was held by the Jerusalem church. As a Hellenist (a person who is Greek in language, outlook, and way of life, but not in ancestry), he could appreciate the feelings of the Greek believer. As a Levite, he understood Jewish biases. All members of the Jerusalem church had confidence in Barnabas' ability to evaluate the new movement properly and to decide if it was of God. Their trust was not misplaced. He saw that a new era had arrived; these Greeks had become believers without first submitting to Jewish ceremonialism. Without a house-top vision, he recognized the hand of God in the Antioch revolution. Had he been narrow-minded, he might have accused the new church of being heretical. But Barnabas' supportive view enabled him to anticipate the decision of the first church council by years.

Seeing the grace of God at work, "he was glad and encouraged them all to remain true to the Lord with all their hearts" (Acts 11:23, NIV). Luke sums up his character in meaningful words, "He was a good man, and full of the Holy Spirit and faith" (11:24, NIV). The result of Barnabas' verdict was an ingathering of souls. The record states "a great number of people were brought to the Lord" (11:24, NIV).

It was at Antioch that believers were first called Christians. It was the Antioch church which commissioned the missionaries who brought the Gospel to Europe. The gate was opening for the evangelization of the world because bigotry had not shut the door. What far-reaching results proceeded from the faithful exercise of Barnabas' gift of encouragement.

He Coached a Promising Worker

Barnabas soon saw that he could not handle the situation at Antioch by himself. He needed a qualified associate. He recalled the young, zealous scholar whose conversion he had vouched for at Jerusalem. Paul's abilities to teach, his exceptional education at the feet of Gamaliel, a famous Jewish teacher, and his Greek background were just the answer.

Barnabas took no chance with a messenger but set out himself for Paul's home city, Tarsus. There, Paul had found a haven from the harassment of Jerusalem leaders who were angered at the loss of their champion to the despised "Way." Though doubtless engaged in some limited service in Tarsus, Paul may have been chafing at his relative inactivity, often wondering when the commission given him on the Damascus Road to bring the Gospel to Gentiles and kings would ever begin to be fulfilled. Barnabas brought Paul to Antioch as his associate. By so doing Barnabas performed a notable service for Paul, bringing him out of obscurity and into the arena of his major ministry.

Barnabas has been called "a good man behind a great man." Throughout history many great men have been helped by someone like Barnabas. Late on a summer afternoon in 1536 John Calvin, already a famous scholar and author of the classic, *The Institutes* at the age of twenty-seven, came by chance to Geneva, Switzerland. On his way to make his home at Basel, haven of scholars and thinkers, he had taken the roundabout way through Geneva since the direct route to Basel had been cut off by war. He intended to rest for the night at the village inn there. When William Farel, leader of the Reformation party at Geneva, learned that Calvin was staying at the inn, Farel hurried to the inn to convince Calvin to remain and carry on the work of the Reformation in Geneva. Calvin protested that he was looking forward to a period of retirement and study at Basel and that he was poorly fitted to lead the battle for the Reformation. The impetuous Farel replied, "You trouble about nothing else than your studies. Well, then, in the Name of the Almighty, I tell you that unless you give ear to His call, your plans He will not bless. May God curse your studies if, in such urgent need, you dare hold back and refuse to give help and support!" Calvin bowed his head in assent (Clarence McCartney, *The Wisest Fool and Other Men of the Bible,* Abingdon-Cokesbury, pp. 53-54). Just as Farel, Calvin's encourager, has faded in the presence of Calvin's brilliance, so has Barnabas been eclipsed by the magnificence of Paul.

By trying to do everything himself and forgetting the capable teacher at Tarsus, Barnabas could have reigned as sole leader at Antioch. But the welfare of the church, not his own position, was his driving passion. He knew intuitively that ultimately Paul's abilities would give him the ascendancy, yet the thought of one day giving way to Paul's leadership did not disturb Barnabas.

And the day came. On the first missionary journey Paul's explosive power over sorcerer Elymas probably surprised Barnabas; however, he showed no sign of resentment as he saw the tremendous energy of his fellow-worker (Acts 13:8-12). Later, in the synagogue in Pisidian Antioch it was Paul who responded to the invitation to speak. No longer was it "Barnabas and Paul" but rather "Paul and Barnabas." Luke's later omission of Barnabas' name further emphasizes Barnabas' declining status: "Paul and his company put out to sea from Paphos and came to Perga in Pamphilia" (Acts 13:13). Without envy, Barnabas recognized the superiority of Paul. The senior partner was willing to let the junior partner take over top billing. A Christian shows maturity when he can become assistant to his assistant and carry on with undiminished enthusiasm. Someone wrote: "It takes more grace than I can tell to play the second fiddle well." Barnabas was like John the Baptist, forerunner of Jesus, who said, "He must increase, but I must decrease."

How grateful I am for the Christian businessman who, as presiding elder in a Brethren assembly, sensed my call to the ministry and invited me, as a teenager, to deliver a sermon in his Sunday evening service. Though I didn't do too well the first time, he invited me back more than once, helping to launch me on a ministerial career.

He Rescued a Young Defector

Interestingly, the sharp argument that eventually split Paul and Barnabas issued from Barnabas' gift of encouragement. Recognizing in his nephew Mark a potential leader just as he had in Paul, Barnabas took Mark on the first missionary journey as an assistant. But before the journey was half over, Mark left Paul and returned home.

When the time came for another missionary tour, sharp contention arose between Paul and Barnabas over taking John Mark with them. Paul thought of the work, Barnabas of the man. Paul operated on the principle—why endanger the work by taking along the man who failed us last time? But

Barnabas considered the person—why not grant this promising young man another chance?

Who was right—Paul or Barnabas? People have debated
the answer to this question for centuries. Perhaps the attitudes of both men were needed to help Mark grow up spiritually. Paul's refusal made Mark realize that somehow he
would have to redeem himself. Barnabas' willingness to take
Mark along, even if it meant losing his friendship with Paul,
made Mark desperately want to prove himself. Uncle Barnabas' sympathetic insistence on giving Mark another chance
helped rescue Mark for future service. Otherwise, Mark's
potential for the ministry, which Barnabas saw so clearly,
might have been wasted.

An interesting uncle-nephew relationship was featured in
the *New York Times* Sports section on June 2, 1986. The
front page story focused on Gary Sheffield, a player on a
high-school baseball team in Tampa, Florida. Sandy Johnson,
assistant general manager of the Texas Rangers, said, "He's
one of the top, if not *the* top high school player in the
country." Sheffield was expected to be a top choice in the
1986 baseball draft. Interestingly, Sheffield is a nephew of
Dwight Gooden, star pitcher for the New York Mets.

When Gooden was 12 and Sheffield was 8, their two families lived together temporarily, and the two boys shared the
same bedroom. Though officially it was an uncle-nephew
relationship, actually they were more like brothers. They
made a big old field in the back into a baseball diamond,
building a backstop with bricks. Even then Gooden was devoted to the game from daybreak to dusk. "He'd wake up
early, take a bath, and eat," Sheffield recalled. "He would
wake me up and make me go to the field without taking a
bath or eating. I used to want to go eat, and he wouldn't let
me. He used to hit the ball real hard." The 12-year-old
would hit dozens of ground balls that would bounce off

rocks or holes and into the 8-year-old's legs, chest, and face.

Gooden explained, "I wanted him to do the same thing I intended to do—play baseball. But he wasn't really into it, so I just kind of demanded it. I used to throw the ball up and hit it. It would bounce and hit him in the face. He'd cry, and I'd make him stay out there."

But Sheffield could also remember when his uncle advanced through Little League to the major league. He recalled how his uncle got a complete uniform with pants and stirrups. Said Sheffield, "I thought that was a big thing. He said if I did good, he'd let me wear his uniform." But what Sheffield remembers most is the 1982 draft, the day the Mets made Gooden their fifth choice. That's when Sheffield began to look at the game of baseball a little differently, "like a job," he said. If Sheffield ever makes the majors, he'll certainly be indebted to his uncle's encouragement.

He Prompted Writers of the New Testament

If Barnabas had not used his gift of encouragement, we might be missing half the New Testament books. By rescuing Mark, he secured a writer of one of the four Gospels. This Gospel has been a source of great blessing in its portrait of Christ as Servant. Through his cultivation of Paul, Barnabas also influenced the writer of 13 epistles. Barnabas himself never wrote a book that found its way into the sacred canon, but he encouraged two men who between them wrote 14 books, over half of the 27 New Testament volumes. How much we owe this self-effacing encourager!

3. Mark, the Restored

A pastor on the West Coast relates his burden for another pastor who had moved into the community to begin life over as a watchman in a mill after he had been dismissed by his denomination for immorality. The former minister and his wife attended this pastor's church, and the two men became good friends, often having lunch together. The pastor urged the watchman to accept the forgiveness which he professed to have sought and which he had preached for several years. But the guilt-laden watchman found this difficult because he believed that God has a separate standard for ministers. Occasionally, the pastor invited the watchman to minister for him. In time, the watchman came to accept the fullness of God's gracious pardon. Later, his denomination recognized the change in him, officially reinstated him, and offered him a small church to start his ministry anew.

The day the reinstated minister was to leave for his new charge, he told his pastor friend he had changed his mind: "After what I did in my last church, I don't deserve another chance." This confession sent the pastor to his knees on behalf of his friend. With eyes closed in prayer, he envisioned a large room lined with books alphabetized by names of people. A large hand with an extended index finger began to move across the books until it came to one with the watchman's name on it. The book was opened so it could be read. The early pages told of his childhood years, marriage, and first years in the ministry. But where the book should have recorded the episode of his immorality, the page was absolutely blank. Then came the recording of his repentance with a marginal note of rejoicing in heaven. The following pages told of his reinstatement and call to the new church. On the bottom of the erased page were the initials, *J.C.* Jesus Christ had blotted out the charges against him.

After this vision the excited pastor hurried to phone the watchman. Hearing what his friend had visualized in prayer, the watchman quit his job at the mill, accepted the new church position, and reentered the ministry with renewed determination to serve his Lord faithfully. (Dean Merrill, *Another Chance,* Zondervan, pp. 117-120).

John Mark, a member of the Other Twelve, was also given another chance to prove himself faithful. Related to Barnabas, he was not a surprising choice as a helper to Barnabas and Paul on their first missionary journey. But for whatever cause, Mark left his companions part way into their mission and went home. Because of this, Paul absolutely refused to take Mark on a proposed second missionary trip with Barnabas: "He deserted us. He's not reliable."

Barnabas insisted on taking Mark along on a separate mission to Cyprus. How would Mark respond to this second chance? Was his career really finished?

About 15 years later these questions were answered. Mark's career was flourishing. In his final recorded words, not long before his execution, Paul requested Timothy to bring Mark, "for he is profitable to me for the ministry"

(2 Tim. 4:11). Furthermore, we find Mark in the company of Peter, from whom he learned much of the material that went into the second book of the New Testament (1 Peter 5:13).

This Christian worker, given a second chance, was the one chosen by the Holy Spirit to pen the exciting, drama-packed life of Christ, known as the Gospel of Mark.

He Came from a Godly Home

John was his Jewish name; Mark was his Roman name. The mention of the two names (Acts 12:25) coincides with his entrance into the company of Barnabas and Saul and ministry in the great Gentile city of Antioch. Perhaps his Roman name indicated Roman citizenship, a supposition quite consistent with the status of his family.

His mother was Mary who apparently owned her own home, leading us to surmise that her husband was deceased. Like many industrious Jews, perhaps she and her husband had become rich in the outside world, then retired to Jerusalem, headquarters for their nation and their religion. Mary was sister to Barnabas of Cyprus, who likewise was a person of wealth (Col. 4:10; Acts 4:36).

The description of her house signaled her wealth. The house had a gate and a passageway leading to the inner court. Her home had room enough for a considerable crowd. Many gathered there to pray for Peter's release from prison (Acts 12:12). The mention of a servant girl who answered the door is a further hint of a well-to-do home.

If Mary's house had been a center of social importance before she became a follower of Jesus, how natural for her to make it a place of Christian activity. Many Bible scholars think Mary's home was the upper room where Jesus celebrated the Last Supper, where the 120 gathered for prayer after the Ascension, and where the tongues of fire descended on the Day of Pentecost (Acts 1:13; 2:2). Mary laid her gift of hospitality at the feet of Jesus. Breaking away from her strong Levitical background, she threw her lovely, spacious home open to Christ's people. Undoubtedly, her home was one of the many house-churches in which the thousands of early believers met in Jerusalem. How wonderful when the rich use their wealth and social standing for the service of Christ.

He Found Himself in the Circle of Christian Leaders
Mark may well have been one of the followers of Jesus during His earthly ministry. He is thought to be the young man who followed Jesus after His arrest in Gethsemane, and when seized by young men of the arresting mob, left his linen cloth and fled, naked. Significantly, Mark is the only one of the four Gospel writers who records this incident (Mark 14:51-52).

With his mother's home a haven for believers, Mark became acquainted with leaders like Peter, James, John, and the other members of the Twelve. As a boy, Billy Graham met evangelists in much the same way that Mark met the apostles. Whenever evangelists pitched their tents in Charlotte, North Carolina, a crossroads for itinerant preachers, Billy Graham's mother invited these revivalists to dinner, exposing her son to such men on a first-name basis. He grew up hearing their supper-table stories of how they had swayed vast audiences through the South.

Mark seems to have had a special relationship with Peter. By calling Mark "his son," Peter indicates that he led young Mark to become a follower of Jesus (1 Peter 5:13). It was to Mark's home that Peter gravitated the night he was miraculously released from prison. A large crowd had gathered there to pray all night for Peter's release. When his chains were knocked off his hands, the iron gate opened to the city, and the reality of it all dawned on him, Peter went "to the house of Mary the mother of John, whose surname was Mark; where many were gathered together praying" (Acts 12:12). Mark, an interested spectator that night, would readily recall how none of them believed the servant girl, Rhoda, but in unbelief left Peter knocking at the door. Finally Rhoda opened the door, and the crowd inside Mary's home was astonished to see him.

Mark traveled on mission tours with Peter and likely learned much of the material for his Gospel from talks with that great proclaimer of the faith.

He Received a Special Invitation

Barnabas and Paul brought Mark back from Jerusalem to Antioch after fulfilling their relief mission (Acts 12:25). To be in the company of these two great men was an unusual privilege for Mark.

What an honor a little later to be invited by the same two leaders to accompany them on their first missionary journey. Barnabas and Paul had just been officially set apart by the Holy Spirit and the church to carry the Gospel to other areas (Acts 13:1-3). They needed a helper, so they approached Mark.

What kind of help did Mark give? The word *minister* describing his function in Acts 13:5 meant literally "an underrower," a rower with others above him in the boat. Gradually, the word came to mean minister, attendant, helper. Synagogues had attendants like the one who handed Jesus the scroll when He read the Scripture in his hometown (Luke 4:20). Many suggestions have been made as to the nature of Mark's service. He might have:
- helped in the preaching service,
- instructed the new converts,
- baptized new believers,

- arranged for board, lodging, and travel like an advance agent for an evangelistic team,
- served as a secretary, handling business details.

Mark was a supernumerary. As an extra, he had not been officially set apart and commissioned like Barnabas and Paul. He is brought to our attention in an incidental manner. As Barnabas and Paul explained how they needed him, the very novelty of going out on this adventuresome mission with these two great men would appeal to Mark, especially since the leadership of the affair seemed to be under his own flesh and blood relative. Although his mother's heart may have fluttered when she heard he had been invited, she encouraged him to accept. Unfortunately, Mark embarked on this journey without a firm committal to the ministry as a life-calling. (He probably was around 30 years of age at this time.)

He Deserted Paul and Barnabas Suddenly

They had just sailed from the island of Cyprus to the city of Perga on the south side of Asia Minor, still in the very early stages of their projected mission, when suddenly, "John left them and returned to Jerusalem" (Acts 13:13, NASB). Scripture contains no mention of anyone coaxing the junior member to stay on.

Why did Mark defect? Some biblical scholars suggest:

- He felt homesick, maybe missing a girlfriend back in Jerusalem or Antioch.
- He worried about his mother's well-being and about neglecting his duties at home.
- He desired to rejoin Peter.
- He suffered from seasickness or insect bites.
- He realized that the change in route due to an illness Paul suffered meant he would be away from home a longer time than he wanted to be. (Because of Paul's

Mark, the Restored

illness, they had to go to the healthier climate of the interior instead of visiting the seaports on the western coast of Asia Minor.) This change in plans would also mean traversing difficult and dangerous mountains rumored to be infested with robbers. Mark wasn't yet ready to endure hardships as a good soldier of Jesus Christ.

The most frequent of all suggestions for Mark's defection is the loss of Barnabas' leadership to Paul. Barnabas had been the preeminent one for several years. Barnabas had been a believer before Paul. Barnabas had been the one to vouch for the validity of Paul's conversion when the church leaders were skeptical. Barnabas had been the father figure in the Antioch church, nurturing it along. Barnabas had been the one who sought out Paul and rescued him from obscurity by giving him a vital ministry at Antioch. Barnabas had been the leader of the team as they started this first missionary tour. Now Paul was taking over. At Paphos on Cyprus when Sergius Paulus became a believer, Paul had stepped to the forefront. The old order changed. Instead of writing *Barnabas and Paul,* Luke records it as *Paul and Barnabas* (Acts 13:42). Perhaps Mark could not bear to see his uncle take second place.

Closely related to Mark's resentment over Paul's ascendancy is thought to be Paul's aggressive attitude in evangelizing Gentiles. Mark may have been uneasy about evangelizing Gentiles. We know that even Barnabas had misgivings in this area, for Paul had to rebuke him on one occasion for separating himself from Gentile believers (Gal. 2:13). Nothing irritated Paul so deeply as any suggestion that a Gentile needed to submit to Jewish ordinances in order to be saved. Some biblical scholars see in Paul's strong refusal to take Mark on a second journey a hint of Mark's lack of sufficient enthusiasm for Gentile evangelism.

From Paul's attitude we gather that he felt Mark had no legitimate reason for turning back. As far as he was concerned, Mark had put his hand to the plow and looked back and was thus unfit for kingdom service. Even Mark's mother must not have been thrilled to see her son come home so soon, especially when she learned the facts. Mark soon found himself in an embarrassing position.

In the spring of 1986, just as missions agencies were putting the finishing touches on their overseas short-term summer programs, media attention was focused on international terrorism. Libya had just been bombed for several alleged acts of terrorism.

Missionary News Service conducted a survey to see how this incident affected missions programs. The survey, published by Evangelical Missions Information Service, reported that eight organizations who have operated summer programs for several years did not have any program cancellations.

Some groups did, however, experience slightly higher than normal cancellation rates among their recruits. Others reported that their quotas, even for programs in so-called risk areas, were already filled. Many agencies were still receiving first-time applications for open positions.

Greater Europe Mission reported that "every time a bomb goes off, the phone rings." Seven people canceled in ten days. But some calling were new applicants. Some said, "We're going anyway. Khadaffi isn't going to stop us." The general conclusion of the survey was that terrorism would not drastically curtail the summer programs which have become a major part of many missionary organizations.

Some of these short-term missionary candidates, like Mark, defected from their obligation. Others, like Mark, had a chance to think things over, repent, and renew their commitment.

Mark Has a Change of Heart

Paul and Barnabas returned triumphantly from their missionary journey, reporting the people saved and the churches planted, emphasizing the opening of the door of faith to the Gentiles (Acts 14:27). About a year later Paul suggested a second missionary journey to see how the brethren were progressing in the cities where he and Barnabas had previously preached the Word. Paul did not invite Mark. How could one who had forsaken him in time of need be trusted in moments of danger, especially when confronted by an angry mob?

What were Mark's thoughts as he had to live with the fact that one of the world's bravest saints considered him a quitter and a deserter, unfit to accompany him on his missionary journey?

Probably, Mark was never fully happy after leaving Perga, especially on hearing reports of all God accomplished through Paul and Barnabas after his defection. He learned that the church council at Jerusalem decided Paul was correct in evangelizing Gentiles. Peter, Mark's hero, had testified that Gentile conversion needed no Judaistic ceremony to complete it. Any prejudice Mark might have had against preaching salvation to the Gentiles disappeared. Gradually, he had also come to accept Paul's leadership over Barnabas.

Some in Mark's shoes, rejected by Paul, would have reacted with angry defiance and fallen into deeper shame. But to his credit Mark resolved in his heart to show Paul, by faithfulness to the Lord in his future course of life, that he could make a man out of himself yet. Mark, who started so ignominiously, intended to finish well. Though he tossed away his first opportunity, he would make good use of his second chance.

The story is told of a man, like Mark, who lost out on his first opportunity, but made good on his second chance. This man told how after his father died, he lived alone with his mother, a wonderful woman and avid reader who slowly began to lose her sight. "She wanted me to stay home and read to her evenings, but I was running around with a gang. Staying home with my mother wasn't exciting for me. One night I found her dead in her chair and on her lap lay an open book, which I knew she couldn't see well enough to comprehend."

With that sight indelibly printed on his memory, this man didn't care what happened to him after that and soon landed in prison. He would gladly have given the rest of his life just to spend one evening reading to his mother, but it was too late. Some time after his release from jail, driving through his hometown, he noticed a sign for a convalescent home. He stopped at the home and asked the lady at the desk if anyone there would like to be read to. The clerk replied with astonishment, "There's an elderly lady here who loves to read but is going blind. I'll take you to her."

Sitting with an open book on her lap was a woman who handed him the book as though she had been expecting him. He read to her. For the next few weeks he visited her often and read to her each time. While reading one night, he sensed something had happened. Looking up, he saw that she had passed away. For a fleeting moment she took on the form of his mother. He blinked his eyes, and the figure in front of him was once again the lady he had been visiting. Immediately, all the remorse he had suffered since his mother's death disappeared.

Mark and Paul Are Reconciled
Mark's defection didn't seem like permanent desertion to Barnabas. Paul was not convinced. Barnabas pled Mark's case. Paul turned him down. With his characteristic generous attitude, Barnabas gave Mark another chance, though it

meant painful separation from his companion of several years. So supportive was Barnabas that he sailed off with Mark on their own mission, letting Paul pick another worker for his second missionary journey.

Mark is not mentioned in the New Testament for the next decade. Tradition says he went as a missionary to Egypt and founded the church at Alexandria, but what really happened in the interim we do not know. We do know that Mark was faithful in his association with Barnabas; moreover, he was a steadfast and valuable companion to Peter. As soon as Mark proved that he could behave better than he had at Perga, surely Paul must have told Mark that all was forgiven. After all, hadn't Paul penned those words, "Brethren, if a man be overtaken in a fault, ye which are spiritual, restore such an one in the spirit of meekness; considering thyself, lest thou also be tempted" (Gal. 6:1). The toughness of Paul along with the tenderness of Barnabas helped bring about this reconciliation. Mark had wholly recovered Paul's good esteem. Paul now watched Mark's career with deep interest and increasing joy.

The next time Mark is mentioned we find him with Paul in his first imprisonment at Rome. Their differences have long since been resolved. Mark is one of Paul's few remaining loyal workers (Col. 4.10; Phile. 24). In the Colossians reference Paul recommends Mark to the saints at Colossae. He writes, "You have received instructions about him; if he comes to you, welcome him" (Col. 4:10, NIV). Apparently, Paul's earlier low opinion of Mark had spread around to a wide area of churches. Since the Colossian church regarded with suspicion the man who once deserted him, Paul seems to be reinforcing a previous communication in which he had set the record straight about Mark. He asks them to welcome Mark if he comes. Thoughtfully, Paul wishes to make sure that Mark's past will not be held against him, so Paul grants him unqualified endorsement as one of his faithful friends. Paul's action speaks highly of both Paul and Mark.

Even a greater tribute is paid Mark in Paul's last recorded letter, written from the dreaded Mamertine prison in Rome not long before his execution. Paul asks Timothy to bring the cloak left behind at Troas and the books and parchments. He wants Timothy to come before winter. His friends have gone on various missions so that only Luke is with him. He adds one more request: He has a friend he wants Timothy to bring. Of all Paul's vast list of companions who will it be? It's Mark! "Take Mark, and bring him with thee: for he is profitable to me for the ministry" (2 Tim. 4:11). As Paul faced execution, he wanted with him the quitter who deserted him in an hour of need at the foothills of the Galatian mountains. Now Mark is useful for ministering. What crowning words! The man who failed at first has made good.

Mark Thrives as Peter's Son in the Faith

Whenever Dr. William Ward Ayer, the pastor responsible for my entering the ministry, wrote a book, he would send me a copy inscribed, "To my son in the faith." In a similar tone Peter refers to Mark as his son (1 Peter 5:13). Peter likely led Mark to Jesus.

Tradition says that Mark was an attendant, interpreter, and close friend of Peter. Mark was likely with Peter during most of A.D. 50–60 right up to the apostle's martyrdom. As Peter's secretary, he may well have transcribed Peter's two epistles with Silvanus serving as bearer of the letters (1 Peter 5:12). Mark had long been approved in the eyes of Peter who, because of his own denial of Jesus and later restoration, could so easily sympathize with Mark.

Christian scholarship and tradition maintain that Mark

received much of the material in his Gospel from Peter. Of course the Holy Spirit inspired Mark, but the Spirit also provided some of the material from Mark's relationship with Peter. Only an eyewitness could have provided some of the details such as mention of a pillow on which Jesus was sleeping during the violent Galilean storm or the singling out of Peter to be told by the angels of Jesus' resurrection that first Easter morn (Mark 4:38; 16:7). Peter was a man of action; therefore, Mark was influenced to present his Gospel vividly and with the speed of a motion picture. The word translated *immediately, forthwith,* or *straitway,* occurs approximately 40 times in Mark, more than in all the rest of the New Testament books combined.

Mark presents Christ as Servant. Only four parables are recorded in Mark in contrast to numerous recorded miracles. This fits the character of a servant who is supposed to be doing rather than speaking. Mark's Gospel, more than the other three, emphasizes the eyes of the Lord looking around, and the hands of the Lord ministering. Is not a servant supposed to look around to see what should be done, then do it?

How fitting that he who was a helper wrote the "servant" Gospel. And how fitting that he who flunked at the beginning made good after failure, so much so that the second book in the New Testament bears his name. Mark blundered, but his name is known the world over as the author of the second Gospel. Today, those who fall should take courage, as should those who try to restore the fallen.

4. James, the Lord's Brother

Dr. V. Gilbert Beers, a Senior Editor for *Christianity Today* and one of the luncheon speakers at the 1985 NAE Annual Convention in Columbus, Ohio, began his talk on the family by referring to a woman he had never met, but who had shaped the lives of all members of his family for four generations. She was his wife's grandmother.

Wife of a struggling, small-town Lutheran pastor expecting the birth of their fourth child, she was suddenly widowed. Her husband left her totally penniless. She was so poor that to survive she had to move in with her brother. Now, with four small children, no way to earn money to feed them, and no nice clothing, she became totally dependent on her brother.

According to Dr. Beers, "In her nothingness she decided on a mission for her life. That mission would be to pray for the salvation and spiritual growth of her four children and her unborn grandchildren and great grandchildren. And Grandma believed her prayers would be answered, so she wholeheartedly devoted her entire life to fulfilling her mission of prayer. That was four generations ago."

Dr. Beers continued, "I had the privilege of knowing all four children after they grew up. All bore the aura of the presence of Christ in their lives. To be with them was to be with the Saviour. I could never appreciate a mother-in-law joke because one of those daughters became my mother-in-law."

Of the 17 people in his wife's generation, one became a missionary to Africa, another a missionary to Japan, and another a trustee of a Christian college, a man whose whole mission was to earn money to give away to Christian work. Everyone in this third generation was dedicated to Jesus Christ and establishing a Christian family.

Again, in the fourth generation everyone was a dedicated Christian; all married believers and raised Christian families. All Grandma's descendants look on her as the source of a great heritage even though many have never met her. She has shaped the lives of generations and will continue to do so. Dr. Beers concluded, "Grandma lived what she preached to her family and had the simple audacity to believe God would answer her prayers."

Like this grandmother, Jesus must have prayed long and often for the salvation of His family. For years they never believed in Him but rather mocked Him, even thinking Him out of His mind. Perhaps Jesus spent many of those late night and early morning hours of prayer in earnest intercession for the salvation of his family. One of His brothers, James, not only came to believe in Him, but also took over the leadership of the church at Jerusalem and authored a New Testament book.

James Was the Lord's Brother
Paul refers to *James, the Lord's brother* (Gal. 1:19), as one of the leaders of the church at Jerusalem. Because the New

Testament repeatedly makes a distinction between the disciples of Jesus and His brothers (Matt. 12:46-49; John 2:12; 7:3; Act 1:13-14, 1 Cor. 9:5), this James who is the Lord's brother could not have been one of the twelve disciples, either James, brother of John, or James, son of Aphaeus.

This James was one of Jesus' four brothers, all mentioned by name in two Gospels. When Jesus returned to His home community, the local people, amazed at His wisdom and miracles, remarked, "Is not this the carpenter's son? Is not His mother called Mary? And His brethren, James, and Joses, and Simon, and Judas? And His sisters, are they not all with us?" (Matt. 13:55-56). Mark 6:3 also mentions Jesus' brothers and sisters.

Some, wishing to maintain the perpetual virginity of Mary, hold that these brothers and sisters were really step-brothers and step sisters, children of Joseph by a previous marriage. Others argue that brother and sister here really means "cousin." But it seems evident that Mary bore other children. Matthew writes that Joseph did not have sexual relations with her *until* she had delivered "her firstborn son" (1:25). Luke also writes of Mary delivering "her firstborn son" (2:7). If Mary never had other children, shouldn't Matthew and Luke have said "her *only* son"? The natural meaning indicates that James was the son of Joseph and Mary. Jesus was miraculously virgin-born, but James was of natural descent.

Imagine the happiness of this home as the sons and daughters came one by one and passed through the various stages of infancy, childhood, adolescence, and young manhood and womanhood. James had the model of a perfect elder brother who was obedient to His parents and who set a perfect example of godly living. James saw incarnate holiness in every stage of life. As we shall see later, the influence of Jesus ultimately left a profound mark on James.

James Practiced Humility

James never made capital of his relationship to Jesus. He simply identifies himself at the beginning of his epistle as "James, a servant of God and of the Lord Jesus Christ" (1:1). He gives Jesus His full title, "Lord Jesus Christ," but in all modesty plays down his flesh and blood connection with Him.

He could have written, "We played together. We worked in the same carpenter shop. We went to the synagogue together every Sabbath. We traveled together to Jerusalem every year to celebrate the Passover. He made a special appearance to me after His resurrection. He wanted me to be the leader of the church at Jerusalem." But James was silent about such claims, styling himself not the *brother* but the *slave* of his Master.

Years ago I wrote a story on a Bible college president. He never once mentioned to me that he was brother-in-law to the governor of California. I happened to discover this interesting fact by chance while interviewing one of his friends.

James seems to have exercised similar humility by failing to mention his kinship with the Saviour. He certainly earned the right to pen in his epistle such words as, "God resisteth the proud, but giveth grace unto the humble," and "Humble yourselves in the sight of the Lord, and He shall lift you up" (4:6, 10).

James Eventually Believed

James and his brothers did not believe on Jesus during His lifetime. His mother, Mary, ever mindful of His miraculous conception, the visits of the shepherds and the wise men, and the demonstration of her 12-year-old's wisdom in dialoguing with the temple doctors, had no trouble accepting His claims. But His brothers reacted differently. Perhaps at first they rejoiced in His miracle of turning water into wine at Cana of Galilee, for they seemed in good fellowship immediately following the wedding as they journeyed to Capernaum (John 2:12).

We cannot put our finger on the origin of their distrust, nor trace its undeniable growth. By the time Jesus returned to His hometown and spoke in the synagogue there, His brothers and sisters likely shared the popular resentment of Him which the populace held (Luke 4:14-29). One time when His friends considered Him mentally unbalanced, His brothers and mother came to shield Him by trying to take Him home (Mark 3:21, 31). Such ill-advised treatment by His own family led Him to assert openly that those who listened to His teachings eagerly and obediently were His real family. His actual words were, "Who is My mother, or My brethren? For whosoever shall do the will of God, the same is My brother, and My sister, and mother" (Mark 3:33, 35).

Still later, just before the Feast of Tabernacles, His brothers sneeringly suggested that He go to Judea and perform miracles openly, cynical advice which He disregarded. John adds this comment of explanation, "For neither did His brethren believe in Him" (7:3-5).

James may have taken the lead in mocking Jesus. Sadly, those who live at the foot of a beautiful mountain rarely appreciate the glory and grandeur of its peak. Often, we are also unable to estimate the brilliance of our contemporaries. No wonder Jesus said, "A prophet is not without honor, save in his own country, and in his own house" (Matt. 13:57).

Why didn't James believe in Jesus? For 30 years Jesus lived an exemplary life before the other members of the family; they could find no fault in Him. How then do we explain the rejection? Perhaps five factors contributed to it. *First,* could His standards have been too high for them? He would have been severe on every form of evil. He would have practiced avid self-denial. He would have devoted much of his spare time to prayer. They may have found these high standards far too demanding. *Second,* He denounced the religious leaders of the day for their hypocrisy and hardness of heart. *Third,* He welcomed sinners, especially tax collectors who were considered among the scum of society because of their collaboration with the Roman nation and the dishonesty through which many lined their pockets. *Fourth,* He constantly claimed to be the Messiah, the fulfillment of all the Old Testament prophecies of the coming Redeemer. He made such statements as, "Before Abraham was, I am" (John 8:58). He said, in effect, that He would one day raise the dead by the power of His voice and also that all people would stand before Him as Judge. *Fifth,* James might not have been prepared for the suddenness of Jesus' ministry. For 30 years Jesus' life had gone on uneventfully, but now in these last three years He had made such graphic claims. What was it that catapulted Him from the obscurity of a carpenter in a little Galilean town to the status of a rabbi, a prophet, and ultimately, the long-expected Messiah? Perhaps we should not be too hard on James and the others as they puzzled in unbelief over their brother's recent change of behavior.

Eventually, James came to believe on Jesus. Through all the months of James' unbelief, Jesus had His eye on His brother.

An Eastern newspaper related the story of a truck driver who also had a watchful eye. Driving home one evening, a lady noticed a huge truck tailgating her car. When she sped up or slowed down, the truck driver did the same, even when she exited the thruway, and ran through a red light. Panicking, she drove into a service station and screamed for help. The truck driver sprang from his cab, yanked open her back door, and pulled out a man hidden in her backseat.

From his high cab seat the driver had seen the would-be attacker in the woman's car. The chase was to rescue, not to harm her. She had been running from the wrong person.

James too had been running from the wrong person. We are not sure at what point the light broke through. An ancient tradition places James at the last Passover meal. What seems to have solidified James' faith once and for all was Jesus' special appearance to him after the Resurrection. In the great Resurrection chapter, Paul makes a special point to tell us that the risen Christ was seen by James (1 Cor. 15:7). Jesus knew some penetrating ray of light was needed to drive away the smog of doubt, and so He appeared as tenderly to James as He did to Thomas. Perhaps James was filled with remorse for his unbelief, so he needed the consolation of Christ. What a moment when James met the risen Messiah not only as his brother, but also as his Master.

Why did Jesus make a special appearance to James? Having seen the resurrected Christ, James could then influence his brothers and sisters to accept Jesus as their Saviour and Messiah too. Evidently, the brothers were converted immediately, for they were present in the Upper Room with their mother, Mary, and the apostles, all waiting for the power of the Holy Spirit (Acts 1:14).

Because the sisters are not mentioned as being present in the Upper Room, more than one commentator has suggested that they continued in unbelief. But this need not necessarily follow. It's likely that they were all married and living with their husbands back in Nazareth. When the citizens of Nazareth rejected Jesus after His sermon in the synagogue, they remarked, "Are not His sisters here with us?" (Mark 6:3) Apparently they lived in Nazareth. It is likely that James witnessed to his sisters as well as to his brothers, and also won them to faith in Christ.

James' conversion should be an encouragement to all

with longtime unsaved loved ones. Jesus did not win His brothers during His lifetime. Not until after His death do they appear among the believing group. Even the perfect example of Jesus, fortified by His matchless words and powerful deeds, failed to win them while He was alive.

George Müller, a giant of faith known for his answers to prayer, wrote in his diary, "I have been praying every day for 35 years for two men, sons of a friend of my youth. They are not converted yet, but they will be! How can it be otherwise? There is the unchanging promise of Jehovah, and on that I rest." When Müller died his prayer was still unanswered. Within two years of his death, however, one man became a Christian, and it's reported the other was also converted a few years later (Roger Steer, *George Müller: Delighted in God,* Harold Shaw Publishers, p. 267).

I remember seeing a middle-aged man ushering people down the aisle at a friend's church. My friend whispered to me, "That man's father used to usher in this church. He used to ask prayer for his unsaved son, but he died without seeing his prayer answered. Soon after his death, his son became a believer and now ushers people down the identical aisle."

James Became a Leader in Jerusalem

Five events show that James was a top figure in the church at Jerusalem:

1. Peter's release from prison. The night Peter escaped from jail just prior to the morning of his scheduled execution, he arrived at Mary's home where many were gathered in prayer for him. Calming down the astonished saints, he related the details of his miraculous release. Then, before fleeing to a safer environment, he gave this request, "Go show these things unto James, and to the brethren" (Acts 12:17). *Brethren* here means members of the Jerusalem church, and is so translated in the *New English Bible.* This singling out of James implies that by this time he had become an authority in the church there.

2. Paul's visit to Jerusalem three years after his conversion. Immediately after his conversion Paul went to Arabia, then returned to Damascus. "After three years I went up to Jerusalem to see Peter, and abode with him fifteen days" (Gal. 1:18). His purpose was to become better acquainted with Peter. Paul added that he didn't see any of the other apostles except for James the Lord's brother (v. 19). Though not one of the apostles, James bore the title in the larger sense in which it was given to an eyewitness of the risen Christ. The mention of James in the same breath with Peter, and as an apostle in the wider sense, indicates the eminence and authority of James within the Jerusalem church.

3. Paul's visit to Jerusalem 14 years later. After an interval of 14 years, Paul again went up to Jerusalem (Gal. 2:1). On this later visit the leaders of the Jerusalem church confirmed that he preached the true Gospel and gave him the right hand of fellowship, showing unity of message and mission. The leaders Paul mentioned by name as pillars of the church were James, Peter, and John (Gal. 2:9).

4. James' important role at the Jerusalem Council. A party of Christians at Jerusalem, formerly Pharisees, couldn't accept the admission of Gentiles without circumcision into the church. This reactionary party may have thought James was on their side. Wherever they traveled, such as Antioch, they were divisive (Acts 15:1). Paul and Barnabas determined to get this matter settled soon and completely. As representatives of the church of Antioch, they came to Jerusalem, recognized as the administrative center, to engage in a public congress (Acts 15:2-21).

Peter spoke first, championing the view of Paul and Barnabas. He recounted his own experience at Caesarea where the Gentile household of Cornelius received salvation without submitting to circumcision. Then Barnabas and Paul (Barnabas still the more eminent in Jerusalem) related tales of their marvelous successes among the Gentiles on their first missionary journey. Then James, after hearing all sides, gave his decision. If the Judaizers were counting on James, they were sadly disillusioned.

James backed up Peter with an old prophecy from the Book of Amos which foretold that the Gentiles would seek after the Lord. James advised the council to publish a letter declaring that circumcision was not obligatory for Gentile converts, but that they should keep certain Old Testament rules. These rules included abstaining "from pollutions of idols, and from fornication, and from things strangled, and from blood" (Acts 15:20). (Many manuscripts omit the phrase, "from what is strangled," which would then make all the prohibitions from the moral law: idolatry, fornication and bloodshed [murder].) While James was opposed to placing the yoke of Jewish ceremonialism on the necks of Gentile believers, he was not excusing them from obedience to the great moral commands.

It was James who rendered the final verdict. His authority seemed to supersede even Peter's authority. With courage to withstand the Judaizers who probably counted on him to lead their cause, he delivered a decisive decision which would affect biblical liberty for all time. In taking precedence over the apostles, James is again portrayed as an eminent authority in the Jerusalem church.

5. Paul's report to James after the third missionary journey. Bearing an offering from the churches of Greece to the needy, Paul arrived in Jerusalem and was received gladly by the believers (Acts 21:17). The next day to whom does Paul pay a visit? It is to James. All the elders of the church are assembled, probably at James' house, to pay their respects to

Paul and to hear him declare "what things God had wrought among the Gentiles by his ministry" (Acts 21:18-19). Since no apostles were mentioned, it's likely they all were away, fulfilling their mission of preaching the Gospel to other parts of the world. James was in charge.

James and the elders had heard a rumor which had been widely circulated. The report was that Paul taught Jewish Christians not to observe the customs of Moses. Though a lie, many believed it. To allay the false report, the suggestion was for Paul to associate with four men in the temple who, though Christians, were fulfilling the obligations of a Nazirite vow. He was to assume for himself the charges of their vow. The object of the suggestion was to prove to the Jerusalem church that the Judaizers falsified Paul's attitude toward Jewish saints.

The above five considerations demonstrate that James had a leadership position in the Jerusalem church. Would not one of the apostles have been better fitted because of three years training in Jesus' company?

But James may have been nearly 30 years in Jesus' presence, in the same home. Though James didn't accept Jesus' claims until the end of His ministry, this didn't keep him from observing Jesus and listening to His words. Unknown to James, Jesus was indirectly preparing him for a great task ahead.

Not only was James suited for the Jerusalem chief eldership because of His association with Jesus, but he also earned it because of his character. Tradition says that after the Ascension Peter, James the apostle, and John selected James the Just, the Lord's brother, to be the first Bishop of Jerusalem. With the apostles increasingly absent from the holy city, James came to hold the chief position of leadership in the church, whether the correct title be bishop, chief elder, principal minister, or senior pastor.

James Authored a New Testament Book

Though an unbeliever in Jesus before His death, James would have heard His teachings. He must have imbibed many of Jesus' sayings even before Jesus began His ministry. The book of James, traditionally attributed to the brother of Jesus, shows how deeply steeped James was in his elder brother's teachings, not only in content but in phraseology. Scholars have found at least ten parallels to the Sermon on the Mount in this short epistle. Under the inspiration of the Holy Spirit, James was remarkably faithful to his memory of Jesus' teaching. We can't help wondering if some of James' words of wisdom may possibly be some unrecorded utterances of our Lord.

In his New Testament book, James focuses on practical Christian morality. He wants people to be doers of the Word, not hearers only; thus his main emphasis is placed on holy living. James didn't want Jerusalem saints or any other professing Christians to sit in pews on Sunday mornings, mindlessly chanting their hymns or creeds like the parrot who was taught to say, "I love Jesus." For this reason he stressed works.

Because of this emphasis on works, Luther, the champion of faith, called James' letter an epistle of straw. But no real conflict exists between faith and works. Paul deals with the root of salvation which is faith, while James handles the fruit of faith which is works. The works Paul rejects are those which precede salvation and are thus dead. The faith James denounces is one which does not produce good works. Of course, James knows that salvation comes through faith but not apart from works. As Dr. A.T. Pierson put it, "Paul and James do not conflict. They stand not face to face, beating each other, but back to back, beating off common foes" (Herbert Lockyer, *All the Apostles of the Bible,* Zondervan, p. 199). Before anyone disparages the teachings of James, he should realize he is likely disparaging the teachings of our Lord Himself.

Let us note some of the ways James himself was a doer of the Word, practicing what he preached in his epistle.

- James exemplified his teaching on humility (4:6, 10). As stated in an earlier point, he identified himself at the start of the letter in the most modest of terms. He didn't pull rank and speak of himself as a brother of the Lord Jesus Christ, but rather as His slave. He magnified Jesus as the Lord of Glory (2:1) and minimized his own relationship.

- James exemplified his teaching on the tongue (1:19, 26; 3:1-12). During the Jerusalem Council he was swift to hear and slow to speak. Patiently, he listened to the Judaizers, then to Peter, Barnabas, and Paul before expressing his own opinion. He exercised control of his tongue.

- James exemplified his teaching on caring for the poor, the widows, the orphans, and the downtrodden (1:27; 2:1-9; 5:1-8). The church at Jerusalem was known for its sympathy toward its needy. Many members of the church sold possessions and made the proceeds available to relieve the hungry. Though James may not have initiated this program, under his leadership relief through almsgiving certainly did not diminish.

  Also, when Peter, John and James, the brother of Christ, gave Paul the right hand of fellowship on an early visit, they urged him to take the Gospel to the Gentiles and remember the poor (Gal. 2:10). James was probably responsible for this added emphasis and thus indirectly responsible for the offering Paul brought with him after his third missionary journey from the churches of Greece to help the famine-ridden Judean saints.

- James exemplified his teaching on wisdom (3:13-18). His wisdom was displayed in the decision he gave at the Jerusalem Council. He had to satisfy all sides without compromising truth. He certainly upheld salvation apart from any ceremonial obligation, but he reminded Gentile converts that they were still to obey the moral law. His decision seemed to spread calm over troubled waters, illustrating his own words, "the wisdom that is from above is . . . peaceable. . . . And the fruit of righteousness is sown in peace of them that make peace" (vv. 17 and 19). His epistle is the chief wisdom book of the New Testament.

- James exemplified his teaching on prayer (1:5-6; 4:3; 5:14-18). Tradition says that James was a man of prayer. An old writer said of James' pious exercises, "his knees became hard like a camel's because he was always kneeling in the Temple, asking forgiveness for the people."

James was indeed a godly man, reflecting true likeness to Jesus Christ. He died a martyr around A.D. 62 or 63. Tradition says that when he refused to persuade the people to abandon the doctrine of Christ, but rather urged to the contrary, he was thrown down from a pinnacle of the temple. His brains were dashed out with a club. A less colorful account says he was stoned. However he died, he takes his place among the immortal heroes of faith, standing out in bold relief as a major figure of early Christianity.

5. Titus, the Troubleshooter

$\mathbf{A}$ lady who moved to a southern state wrote her former pastor, "We really haven't heard very good reports of the Baptist churches here. There are seven in town because every time people get annoyed with something in the church, they just start another church."

The story is told of church members divided over the question of buying an organ. They argued long and loud over the purchase. When they did vote to buy it, they disagreed over where to put it. Each week it was moved from one side of the sanctuary to the other. One Sunday the congregation arrived to find their new organ missing. Searching the building without success, each side hurled vehement accusations at the other without locating the missing instrument. A year later, and by accident, the organ was found—exactly where it had been all the time—in the covered church baptistry.

The story is also told of two ladies in a train coach who were arguing about the window. One claimed she would die of heatstroke unless it was opened. The other insisted she would die of pneumonia if it wasn't kept closed. The ladies called the conductor who was at a loss to solve the problem. It was then that the stranger sitting with them in the coach spoke up. "First, open the window. That will kill one. Then close it. That will kill the other. Then we'll have peace."

This stranger's solution, though amusing to us, probably angered the two ladies even more. But how wonderful when a person has the knack of stepping into a difficult situation and arbitrating a fair and equitable decision to the satisfaction of both parties. Some business concerns have special men who are gifted in pouring oil on troubled waters. Titus, one of Paul's close companions, seems to have had this gift. Paul sent him on several troubleshooting missions.

Titus, though an outstanding character in the New Testament, is not mentioned by name in the book of Acts. But his name occurs 13 times elsewhere in the New Testament, twice in Galatians, once each in 2 Timothy and Titus, and nine times in 2 Corinthians. Some believe he was a relative of Luke, the author of Acts, and his name was omitted from Acts because of family modesty. Tradition connects Luke's family with Antioch where Titus was probably led to Christ by Paul who called him, "mine own son after the common faith" (Titus 1:4). Titus became a trusted and valuable assistant to Paul who termed him "my partner and fellow helper" (2 Cor. 8:23). Chosen by Paul to transact difficult and delicate business, Titus was capable, tactful, and resourceful in handling such assignments.

Assignment Number One: A Test Case at Jerusalem
The problem at the Jerusalem church was disagreement over the circumcision of Gentiles. Sometime before the Jerusalem Council, Paul and Barnabas made a visit to the

leaders at Jerusalem, bringing Titus with them (Gal. 2:1). They wished to hold a private conference with the older apostles to reach a definite understanding on the admission of Gentiles into the church without first submitting to circumcision. If ceremonial observance was necessary for salvation, then Paul would have felt that his ministry to date had been in vain (2:2). Furthermore, he was contemplating a future ministry that would take him into Asia Minor, so he needed to get a clear understanding with the top brass at headquarters on the message he had previously preached among the Gentiles and intended to keep preaching. Paul did not want the work of evangelization to suffer. He wanted agreement on this vital matter. The problem was complicated by the opposing teaching of the Judaizers who insisted that to be saved Gentiles had to be circumcised.

On this visit to Jerusalem, Paul brought Titus, a Gentile (Gal. 2:3), as "Exhibit A." He was living, examinable evidence of a Gentile who, without coming under the sway of the Mosaic law, could demonstrate fruits of a Spirit-regenerated believer in Christ. Strong pressure was exerted on Paul to circumcise Titus, but Paul felt obligated to refuse. Because a very vital principle was at stake which involved the very heart of the Gospel, Paul was insistent in his refusal. If he had had any inclination to give in, he was prevented by the knowledge that a secret mission of false brethren had been sent like spies to note the liberty of the brethren and to report their complaint with the purpose of enslaving the brethren (Gal. 2:4-5). Paul would not surrender to their demands in the slightest degree, so that the offer of a free salvation could be maintained. Paul put it this way, "We did not give in to them for a moment, so that the truth of the Gospel might remain with you" (Gal. 2:5, NIV).

The resolution. When the apostles saw how the Lord had blessed Paul's ministry, they gave their stamp of approval, only urging him not to forget the needy. Though Paul, not Titus, was the real troubleshooter in this matter of whether or not Gentiles had to submit to the Mosaic law, Titus let himself be the test case, the guinea pig, the ball to be batted or kicked back and forth by the two sides. Titus indeed became part of the troubleshooting process.

Assignment Number Two: Defiance at Corinth

A most casual reading of Paul's first letter to the Corinthians reveals a church full of problems. The church was divided, with various groups pledging allegiance to Paul, Peter, Apollos, and Christ. A man had been sexually involved with his step-mother. Saints were taking each other to court before heathen judges. Believers were eating the Lord's Supper unworthily, some even eating while intoxicated. Many were flaunting their tongues-speaking, disrupting the church services. Some held erroneous doctrine concerning the resurrection of the dead, holding that it was already an accomplished fact. When the situation worsened between Paul and the Corinthians, Paul assigned Titus the task of trying to straighten matters out. Again Titus became a troubleshooter.

To see where Titus entered the fray, let's review the series of chronological steps in Paul's relations with the Corinthian church as some scholars reconstruct it.

- Paul first visited Corinth on his second missionary journey and started the church, ministering there at least a year and a half.
- Paul wrote a letter to the Corinthians telling them "not to company with fornicators." We learn this from a later letter which we know as 1 Corinthians (5:9). No longer in existence, the earlier letter was likely a brief letter directed to the Corinthians alone, not suitable for wider circulation and probably destroyed by the Corinthians. Scholars refer to it as the "previous letter."

- Then Paul wrote 1 Corinthians from Ephesus after learning from visiting the household of Chloe that divisions and immorality were still rife at Corinth despite his previous letter (1 Cor. 1:11). He also addressed some difficulties referred to him in a letter brought by Stephanas, Fortunatus, and Achaicus (1 Cor. 16:17).
- Paul sent Timothy to take care of the grave moral and doctrinal difficulties in the Corinthian church (1 Cor. 4:17; 16:10). Timothy, around 25 and young and timid, was unable to deal with the offenders in the fearless way the situation required. Perhaps this is why Paul later said to Timothy, "Let no man despise thy youth" (1 Tim. 4:12).
- When Timothy returned with a report of little or no progress at Corinth, Paul then made a hurried trip from Ephesus to Corinth himself. Evidently, Paul didn't make much headway in solving the Corinthians' problems on this visit. Their defiance made his stay unpleasant. Scholars call this the "painful visit."
- Now Titus enters the picture. Paul, wishing to avoid another painful confrontation by a personal visit, wrote another letter couched in very severe terms, demanding stern discipline for the unrepentant members of the church. He sent Titus with the letter to try to mediate in the situation. So strong was the letter that Paul almost regretted sending it. Scholars call this the "painful letter." It too has been lost.

Paul's affectionate nature reproached him for sending such a letter. Tortured in conscience, he asked himself if he had been too hard on these new converts. What would their reaction be? Wishing to obtain reliable information as soon as possible, he had instructed Titus to rejoin him at the earliest moment. Evidently Paul regarded the response of the Corinthians to his letter as a crisis in the history of that church. Submission to his authority and discipline of the recalcitrant member or members would mean progress, whereas refusal might mean the destruction of the church.

The resolution. Paul could not wait for Titus to help him. When Paul didn't find Titus at Troas, his restless spirit forced him to forge on toward Corinth, even though great opportunity for Gospel preaching presented itself at Troas. Paul stated, "when I came to Troas to preach Christ's Gospel, and a door was opened unto me of the Lord, I had no rest in my spirit, because I found not Titus my brother: but taking my leave of them, I went from thence into Macedonia" (2 Cor. 12–13). What mixed feelings Paul must have had as he awaited Titus' return.

At last Titus came, bringing news which relieved Paul's anxiety greatly. Their paths crossed somewhere in north Macedonia, perhaps Thessalonica. Titus explained that the majority of the Corinthians, loyal to Paul, had disciplined the flagrant offender, though a small minority still defied Paul's authority. So overwhelmingly overjoyed was Paul that he launched into a doxology (2 Cor. 2:14-17) and didn't mention Titus again until 7:5-6. Titus' mission had been largely successful. Doubtless, Titus had combined love with firmness.

He performed his task with the care of one who washed a brother's feet. To wash a brother's feet is a delicate task. First, we have to make sure his feet are dirty. We should never get the wash basin until we have the facts straight. Paul and Titus had definite information on the Corinthians' need for cleansing.

Next, we should be sure that our own hands are clean. The person who tries to wash a fellow believer's feet with stains on his own hands will botch the job. Titus was a clean vessel, fit for the Master's use.

We should do foot-washing in the proper context. The footwasher should never sound a trumpet before announcing, "I'm about to set Brother X straight." Private wrongs require private correction, and public wrongs demand public correction. For those who sin openly, the command is "rebuke before all" (1 Tim. 5:20). Since the Corinthian sin was an open and flagrant shame, Paul and Titus had to involve the entire church in correcting the wrongs.

Washing feet also requires stooping low. Titus did not come on like a drill officer, nor parade like a peacock on arrival at Corinth. He handled the matter with genuine humility.

Finally, we should dry the washed feet. Without a thorough job of drying, damp feet contacting dirt can make the feet muddier than before the washing. Restoring an erring brother involves drying feet, so he may again walk the paths of righteousness. Titus doubtless forgave and forgot.

F. B. Meyer in his book, *Love to the Uttermost*, says, "We do not often enough wash one another's feet. We are conscious of the imperfections of those around us; we are content to note and criticize them. We dare not attempt to remove them, partly because we do not love with a love like Christ's, and partly because we are not willing to stoop low enough" (Revell, p. 19).

The story is told of some youngsters who won four free goldfish at their school carnival. Their father found an expensive, discarded 10-gallon display tank, complete with gravel and filter for just $5, so he cleaned it up and dropped the fish in their new home. But in a few days all the fish were dead. He discovered his mistake: he had washed the tank with soap which resulted in the death of the very lives he wished to sustain. Someone commented that too often, in cleaning up the lives of others, we use "killer soaps—condemnation, criticism, nagging, fits of temper. Our harsh, self-righteous treatment is more than they can bear."

The manner in which Titus handled the situation at Corinth, however, made for mutual respect and endearment. Paul wrote the church, "his inward affection is more abundant toward you, whilst he remembereth the obedience of you all, how with fear and trembling ye received him" (2 Cor. 7:15). No wonder Paul sent Titus back on another troubleshooting mission.

Assignment Number Three: The Offering at Corinth

A year before the writing of 2 Corinthians, Paul had urged Gentile Christians in Galatia and Macedonia to take an offering for the poor saints in Jerusalem (1 Cor. 16:1-2). The Corinthians had talked loudly about their intent of generosity but had become lax in following through on their intentions. Titus was now assigned the task of reviving and completing the project begun by Paul who wrote, "We desired Titus, that as he had begun, so he would also finish in you the same grace also" (2 Cor. 8:6). The verb *desired* seems to express an assignment (2 Cor. 12:18; 1 Cor. 16:12). Titus accepted the assignment gladly (2 Cor. 8:16-17). He was certified as Paul's personal emissary (8:23) in charge of collecting the Corinthians' subscriptions before Paul arrived.

The resolution. Two of the chapters in 2 Corinthians (8 and 9) have been called the classic passages on Christian giving. Paul surely went over this material with Titus who brought this letter with him, and in turn reviewed it with the Corinthian church. The section begins with a report of the extraordinary generosity of other Macedonian churches which would certainly have included Thessalonica, Berea, and Philippi, the latter known for its repeated financial help to Paul. Their generous giving was all the more remarkable because it was given out of their poverty. Because their contributions exceeded Paul's expectations, he hoped, and

Titus with him, that their example would inspire the Corinthians to excel in giving.

Reviewing Paul's letter, Titus would remind the Corinthians of the supreme example of sacrifice, Jesus Christ, who
gave up the riches of heaven and became poor for our sakes,
that we might gain riches through His poverty (2 Cor. 8:9).
Our willingness to give is what God values. The amount
given varies with each individual's means. At the moment,
the Corinthians seemed to have money to spare to meet the
Jerusalem need. It was hoped that if the Corinthians had a
need someday, the folks in Jerusalem would be able to help
them out (8:12-15).

To avoid any suspicion of misused funds, Titus would also
point out that administrators had been appointed by the
churches to travel with Paul when he came for the offering
(8:19-21). This fear of misused funds also haunts us today.
In many cases generous Americans are bilked out of millions
annually. An article in *Reader's Digest* titled, "Who Really
Gets Your Charity Gift?" discussed how much of a contribu-
tor's donations actually go to the charity's professed goals
and how many dollars line the pockets of the fund-raisers
(Edward Tivnan, May 1984 Reprint).

The Washington-based Evangelical Counsel for Financial
Accountability monitors the fund-raising efforts of its more
than 300 evangelical member organizations which together
receive over a billion dollars annually. The Council requires
each member to hold a responsible board meeting at least
semiannually, undergo an annual audit by an independent
public accounting firm and develop a functioning audit review committee. Each member organization should maintain an available, current audited financial statement and
high standards of integrity. Each member must avoid con-
flicting interests and assure the council that donations are
applied to the stated goals. For decades Billy Graham has

adopted aboveboard methods of finances in all his crusades. He insists that the local committee handle all money, that the books be audited after each crusade and the audit published in the press, and that he receive nothing from the crusade except living expenses while in the city.

After explaining the motivation behind the offering and the careful plans for administering it, Titus would also remind the Corinthians of Paul's principle that sparse sowing would mean minimal reaping, whereas generous sowing would bring bountiful harvest (2 Cor. 9:6).

Then, lest the thought of a collection cause pain, Titus would repeat Paul's statement, "God loveth a cheerful giver" (2 Cor. 9:7). Too often a funeral atmosphere prevails in churches at offering time. Mendelssohn's "Consolation" would be appropriate music to match the mood of many congregations as they bid farewell to their money. But God wishes us to give, not grudgingly, nor because we feel obliged, but cheerfully. Some churches fittingly sing the Doxology as the ushers march down front with the filled collection plates to deposit them on the altar.

Spurred on by Paul's letter and Titus' encouragement, the Corinthians probably responded with an adequate offering.

Assignment Number Four: Things Lacking at Crete

After Paul was released from his first imprisonment at Rome, he took Timothy and Titus with him on further missionary travels. Evangelizing on the island of Crete, favorably located in the center of the Mediterranean, Paul won a large number of converts in many cities, but was called away before he could organize his work. Sending Timothy to Ephesus, Paul left Titus at Crete to "set in order the things that are wanting" (Titus 1:5). This included the selection of qualified church officers, the inculcation of sound doctrine, and the promotion of self-controlled living. In fact, sound teaching and self-restrained conduct are mentioned several times in the epistle.

If the nature of tasks assigned a worker indicates the quality of that worker, Titus emerges with high marks. Already he had successfully completed difficult troubleshooting assignments on behalf of Paul. Now he was asked to "straighten out what was left unfinished" (Titus 1:5, NIV) at Crete, one of the troublesome regions in the Roman Empire, according to references in the literature of the day. Paul described the people of Crete by quoting one of their reputed prophets of six centuries earlier, "Cretans are always liars, evil brutes, lazy gluttons" (Titus 1:12, NIV). So well-known was their deception that the expression "to play the Cretan" was understood to mean "to lie." As to their brutality, the same prophet sarcastically stated that "the absence of wild beasts from Crete was supplied by its human inhabitants" (Charles R. Erdman, *The Pastoral Epistles of Paul,* Westminster, p. 43). Yet Paul was willing to entrust this ministry to Titus.

Immoral, violent living was not confined to the Cretans nor to the first century. Our nation and this decade have witnessed almost unparalleled flagrant sexual license and violent conduct. Dr. Richard C. Halverson, Chaplain of the U.S. Senate, penned the following in his biweekly devotional letter *Perspective* (June 11, 1986).

Animals mate by instinct. . . .
Humans mate by love! God made it that way.
Tragedy is that some humans are like animals. . . .
They mate by instinct! No love! No commitment!
No affection! No intimacy! Just sheer instinct. . . .
Satisfying bodily appetites!
Unfortunately—unlike animals—they do not stop.
Their lust—satiated but never satisfied—drives
them to every conceivable sexual experiment . . .

violence—if necessary.
And when the normal God-given result of mating occurs
—they destroy it like beasts!
What God intended as the most intimate, caring,
loving, selfless relationship—humans degrade to
gross self-indulgence.

The Resolution. Paul's exhortation to the Cretans in his letter to Titus is most appropriate to our generation, "the grace of God . . . teaches us to say 'No' to ungodliness and worldly passions, and to live self-controlled, upright and godly lives" (2:11-12, NIV).

Today's teenagers face challenges much different than those of past generations. Josh McDowell estimates that a typical teenager watches 24 hours of TV a week. During a year, he would see more than 9,200 scenes of sexual involvement. Teenage pregnancy is rampant. McDowell has instituted a massive five-year crusade to make the Christian community aware of the root causes of the teenage sex crisis and to offer positive solutions. He calls his campaign "Why Wait," encouraging abstinence from premarital sex, rather than the use of condoms. This fits Titus' instruction to say no to worldly passion.

God's grace is able to give victory over every type of vice. A visitor at a mission station on a South Sea island was deeply impressed by the spiritual depth of the students, by their personal cleanliness, and by the art that decorated their buildings. But the high point came as he boarded the boat to leave. The girls lined up and sang fervently, "What a wonderful change in my life has been wrought since Jesus came into my heart." What made this song especially moving was the whispered remark of one of the staff members, "Every one of those girls is either the daughter or the grand-daughter of a cannibal!"

Only eternity will reveal how many Cretan lives were transformed through the intervention of Titus' ministry on that island.

6. Silas, the Team Player

At the annual Victor Awards, outstanding players in each major sport are recognized. In 1986 Wayne Gretsky who holds almost every record in hockey won the Victor Award in that sport for the sixth consecutive year. In his acceptance speech, Gretsky remarked that this honor would not be possible if it weren't for his teammates. "The award is really a team effort," said the hockey superstar.

Outstanding athletes in every field acknowledge the indispensability of the other players on their team. In baseball, every winning pitcher reminds over-enthusiastic reporters and fans, "There are eight other men on the field. Without them I couldn't win a single game." In football, running backs and quarterbacks may receive much of the publicity, but without the support of others throwing their unsung but vital blocks, running backs would never score, and quarterbacks would never throw touchdowns.

Silas was a team player. Though we are told nothing of his background or pedigree, we do know he was an important person in the early church community. Tradition says he was one of the 70 whom Jesus sent forth two by two (Luke 10:1). He is best known as Paul's choice for a companion on his second missionary journey. By piecing together bits and hints here and there in Acts and in the Epistles, we are able to get a rather clear picture of Silas as a harmonious partner on at least four teams.

The Team of Jerusalem Leaders

Silas was a Roman citizen. When the magistrates at Philippi learned that in whipping Paul and Silas they had wrongfully beaten Roman citizens and could be fearfully punished, they begged the victims to leave the town (Acts 16:36).

Scholar Sir William Ramsay points out that Roman citizenship was a badge of distinction, and sometimes of moderate wealth. This would give Silas standing among the aristocracy of any provincial town (Herbert Lockyer, *All the Apostles of the Bible,* Zondervan, p. 230). He could more easily meet influential people like the merchant Lydia, honorable women and men of Berea, and Dionysius the Areopagite (Acts 16:14; 17:12, 34).

Silas' Latin name, Silvanus (2 Cor. 1:19; 1 Thes. 1:1; 2 Thes. 1:1; 1 Peter 5:12), would also help gain him entrance into society circles. Roman citizenship along with his spiritual insight would make Silas more sympathetic toward the broader movement of Gentile evangelism. This outlook would also explain his openness to Paul's invitation to be his teammate on his second mission into Gentile territory.

Silas was an important man in Jerusalem. He is characterized as a chief man (KJV) or leader (NIV) among the brothers of that foremost city (Acts 15:22). The verb form gives the idea of ruling, commanding, having authority over. It is translated "governor" in Matthew 2:6, and also in Acts 7:10 where it refers to Joseph as second in command over Egypt. It is used to describe Paul as the chief speaker of the two men the Lystrans thought had come down as gods from heaven (Acts 14:12). The word describes a military leader, or any kind of a supervisor in a controlling or influencing role. The word occurs three times in Hebrews 13 to mean those in charge of the church (7, 17, 24). Though not telling us specifically what his title or office was, author Luke wants us to know that Silas was an important person in the Jerusalem Christian community. If among the 70, or one of Jesus' followers from the early days, he might have been one of those considered for apostleship after Judas' suicide (Acts 1:21-22). If not a leader from the start, he proved himself worthy of shouldering responsibility in the cause of Christ as the years went by. Many think he was one of the Jerusalem elders, a group mentioned in Acts 11:30 and 15:2. By the time he entered the sacred record in 15:22, Silas was held in high repute.

Silas likely shared in those glorious days of the early church, numbered with those who met "daily with one accord in the temple, and breaking bread from house to house, did eat their meat with gladness and singleness of heart, praising God, and having favor with all the people" (Acts 2:45-47). He rejoiced as he saw people saved daily and added to the church. He was probably present when Peter and John, released from prison, reported back to the church, resulting in a powerful prayer meeting (4:23-31).

Silas was a prophet. We do know there were prophets in Jerusalem, such as Agabus who prophesied a coming major famine (Acts 11:27, 28). Though we are never told of Silas prophesying at Jerusalem, we discover him prophesying at Antioch in a situation to be discussed under the next point (15:32). But we can be sure Silas exercised his gift of prophecy in Jerusalem during his many years of ministry there. His prophesying undoubtedly helped project him into a place of prominence in the mother church.

When people hear the word *prophecy,* they often think the word means prediction. But foretelling the future is just a small part of the meaning of prophecy. The English word *prophet* comes from a Greek word, composed of two parts, which means literally—forthtell, to make public. A prophet is a forthteller. Among the many messages he tells forth, some may pertain to the future; thus forthtelling may involve some foretelling, but only incidentally. The main meaning of prophesying is forthtelling. The prophet is God's spokesman, making Him known.

Until the completion of the New Testament and during the Apostolic Age, prophets like Agabus gave special revelations and reliable guidance. But since the completion of the Bible, God's divine written revelation, the gift of prophecy is now identified with proclamation based on the written Word of God. Dr. Earl Radmacher, president of Western Conservative Baptist Seminary, in the school's *Western Communicator* (Fall 1982, p. 2) says,

> In most cases, prophesying simply represents the activity of receiving God's message and passing it on. Before the time the written revelation was complete, the prophet received his message directly from God. Once the writers had inscripturated God's message, however, the preacher as God's spokesman took it from the printed page and heralded it far and wide.

An editorial in *Christianity Today* tells how in Zurich, Switzerland, in the 16th century, it was customary for all ministers and ministerial students to meet five times every week for "prophesying" which means exegetical and systematic expositions of the Bible (Leslie B. Flynn, *19 Gifts of the Spirit,* Victor Books, p. 52).

During those glorious years of early Jerusalem church life

Silas played his part on a team of church leaders in giving Spirit-led guidance. He resisted any temptation to exert his authority independently of other chief men but rather sublimated his place of prominence to the interest of all in order to maintain the unity of the faith, for which, except for a couple of minor blemishes, the church had an excellent record.

The Team of Council Representatives

Silas delivered the council's letter. Silas makes his first appearance in the New Testament record at the end of the first church council. Called to settle the vexing question of Gentile converts needing to submit to the Mosaic ceremonial law for salvation, the council generated heated controversy, threatening a serious breach. The crux of the debate was nothing less than the argument of justification by faith and faith alone or justification by works. After much discussion and testimony by Peter, Barnabas, and Paul, James rendered his verdict. He advised the council to publish a letter declaring that circumcision was not required for Gentile converts, but cautioning them to keep certain Old Testament commands. Here is the letter:

The apostles and elders, your
brothers,

To the Gentile believers in Antioch,
Syria and Cilicia:

Greetings.

We have heard that some went out from us without our authorization and disturbed you, troubling your minds by what they said. So we all agreed to choose some men and send them to you with our dear friends Barnabas and Paul—men who have risked their lives for the name of our Lord Jesus Christ. Therefore we are sending Judas and Silas to confirm by word of mouth what we are writing. It seemed good to the Holy Spirit and to us not to burden you with anything beyond the following requirements: You are to abstain from food sacrificed to idols, from blood, from the meat of strangled animals and from sexual immorality. You will do well to avoid these things.

Farewell (Acts 15:23-29, NIV).

Silas was chosen as a representative. Along with Paul and Barnabas who were going back to Antioch anyway, the Jerusalem leaders and congregation chose two men to join them in an official capacity: Judas surnamed Barsabas, conjectured to be a brother of Joseph Barsabas, who had been nominated for the apostleship lost by traitor Judas (Acts 1:23; Acts 15:22), and Silas. These representatives were to carry the decree to the churches in the concerned areas and to confirm the contents of the decree by word of mouth.

Silas was highly qualified. Along with his fellow representatives, Silas is described among the leading men of the Jerusalem church. He is also declared a brave man who has already risked his life for the Gospel. So when Silas comes on the scene in the New Testament record, he already stands in the forefront, enjoying the unqualified confidence of the mother church. As a Hellenist and a Roman citizen, he represented the more liberal (as related to Mosaic ceremonies) of Jewish believers like Stephen, Paul, and Barnabas. His compatriot, Judas Barsabas, probably represented the more conservative element under the leadership of Peter, James, and John. Both sides, now united against the Judaizers, were represented in these two ambassadors entrusted with this important document.

The choice of Silas as a representative on this important committee shows how highly he was regarded. This was no small mission, but rather one with far-reaching implications with respect to the purity of the Gospel. It required a man with a tactful and peace-loving disposition to handle this delicate matter which could so easily disrupt Jewish-Gentile relationships.

Incidentally, this epistle, carried by the representatives, may be the first Christian letter preserved for us, unless the Epistle of James was written before the Jerusalem Council.

Silas began his ministry at Antioch. It was natural for this team of representatives to make their first report at Antioch. Antioch had been the source and scene of controversy on the question decided by the Jerusalem Council. The third largest metropolis in the Roman Empire with a population of half a million, Antioch was called the gateway to the West and was composed of people from all over the Roman Empire. It was here that Gentiles in large numbers first began to embrace the Christian faith, thus attracting the attention of the church at Jerusalem and prompting the church to send Barnabas to investigate. He found the believers genuine and remained to help them. When the work grew beyond him, he enlisted the help of Paul. It was at Antioch that believers were first called Christians. It was the church at Antioch that sent out the first missionaries who focused on Gentile evangelism. This drew the opposition of Judaizers who claimed Gentile conversion was invalid until completed by circumcision. It was at Antioch where even Peter had wavered on this question. So, how fitting for these messengers to make a beeline for Antioch.

The record says,

So when they were dismissed, they came to Antioch: and

when they had gathered the multitude together, they delivered the epistle: Which when they had read, they rejoiced for the consolation. And Judas and Silas, being prophets also themselves, exhorted the brethren with many words, and confirmed them (Acts 15:30-32).

Not only did they read the letter, but they also amplified it, ratifying the freedom of the Gentile element from the Mosaic ceremonial law, also reinforcing the perfect liberty of the Jewish group to keep ceremonial laws if they wished. Of course they also stressed the obligation of both to obey the moral law as evidence of their genuine faith. Silas exercised the gift of prophecy as described in 1 Corinthians 14:3 by speaking words of "edification, and exhortation, and comfort." One commentator suggested Silas and Judas made "an earnest appeal for unity and mutual charity" (A.T. Robertson, *Types of Preachers in the New Testament,* Doubleday, Doran & Co., p. 137). The congregation heard the message with great delight and was strengthened.

After spending some time there, they were dismissed to report back to the apostles at Jerusalem, yet "it pleased Silas to abide there still" (Acts 15:33-34). This statement is probably an attempt to explain how Silas was in Antioch later when Paul invited him to join his second missionary tour. Silas, however, would have had ample time to make a trip to Jerusalem and return to Antioch before Paul's invitation.

Chosen for Paul's Team
Silas shows such excellent qualities in his ministry in Antioch that Paul, after his separation from Barnabas, decided Silas would make a good partner on his next journey. "Paul chose Silas, and departed, being recommended by the brethren unto the grace of God" (Acts 15:40). The letter containing the decrees made at the Jerusalem Council had yet to be

carried to the churches of Syria and Cilicia. Would not the official representative of the Jerusalem church, Silas, be the logical choice to accompany Paul on such a mission?

As Paul intensified his missionary endeavors and church planting, he surrounded himself with a host of associates, beginning with Silas and later including many others such as Timothy, Tychicus, Ephapharditus, Epaphras, Apollos, Priscilla, Aquila, Demas, and Luke, his personal physician. Paul was a team man, and Silas became a close teammate for most of Paul's second missionary trip.

John H. Glenn was also a team man. When he made America's first orbital flight, circling the earth three times, his spectacular achievement was made possible through the efforts of 30,000 people who participated in the building, launching, tracking, and recovery of the spaceship.

Paul and Silas travel to Philippi. Silas accompanied Paul northwest, pausing at Derbe then Lystra, where Paul conscripted young Timothy for the team, perhaps a substitute for Mark as a general helper. The trio went from town to town in Asia Minor, delivering "the decrees for to keep, that were ordained of the apostles and elders which were at Jerusalem" (Acts 16:4). Forbidden to enter Bithynia, they came to Troas where Paul had a vision of a man in Macedonia begging him to come over and help. At Troas, Luke joined the trio, evidenced by using the pronoun *we* instead of *they* in his written account (16:10). Then the missionary quartet, Paul, Silas, Timothy, and Luke, traveled to Philippi where both triumph and trial awaited them. Soon after their arrival, they found a riverside prayer meeting where many women gathered. (Apparently not enough Jewish men lived in Philippi to have a synagogue.) One of the women, a merchant named Lydia, opened her heart to the Lord and opened her home in hospitality to the missionaries. She saw her entire household become believers.

Then came opposition. When Paul cast a demon out of an unnamed slave girl, her owners who received income from her divination lodged false accusations against not only Paul but Silas too. In the opinion of her masters, Silas was equally guilty. No distinction was made between them in the charges and treatment. Both were handled roughly and dragged before the magistrates. Before they could assert their Roman citizenship, which would have exempted them from scourging, they were severely beaten by the cruel Roman lictors. The next day Paul and Silas refused to leave without a dignified dismissal from the magistrates and an apology for their illegal treatment which could easily have gotten these officials into deep trouble with their superiors in the Empire.

Danger was nothing new to Silas. Before he joined Paul, he had been known for having risked his life for the Gospel (Acts 15:26). His conduct, like Paul's conduct, was courageous. Their feet were positioned uncomfortably and tightly in stocks, their backs covered with welts and bruises and coagulated blood, yet "About midnight Paul and Silas were praying and singing hymns to God, and the other prisoners were listening to them" (Acts 16:25, NIV). This strange behavior at midnight, praising God instead of cursing men, won a ready audience in the various cells. This merry pair of singers advertised well how the Christian faith can turn adversity into joy and transform a prison into heaven. An earthquake climaxed the conviction of the jailer already moved by the unusual conduct of these strange prisoners. He fell at the feet of both Silas and Paul (v. 29), asking how to be saved (v. 30). He and his family were baptized and joined the growing church at Philippi. The name of Silas is forever joined with that of Paul in this prison episode. One cannot think of Paul in the Philippian jail without visualizing Silas with him, together exchanging the garment of praise for the spirit of heaviness.

A man who heard General William Booth, founder of the Salvation Army, preach on this conversion of the Philippian jailer forgot much of the message but could never wipe from his memory Booth's climax, "God was so well-pleased with the prayers and praises of Paul and Silas that He cried AMEN with a mighty earthquake" (Lockyer, *All the Apostles,* p. 232).

Silas was not soured by this experience. Though he had been in danger before because of the Gospel, likely he had never been so cruelly beaten for Christ's sake. But it did not deter him in his Christian endeavor and in his partnership in Paul's ministry. Further, he knew that good would come out of this persecution, some of which would be encourage-ment to the new little band of believers in Philippi to be willing to suffer for Christ. A willingness to look for the good that may come out of suffering and disaster is one way to overcome a crisis.

A few years ago when John Hinckley Jr. fired six bullets from a .22 caliber pistol into President Reagan and three others, it might have meant the end of the road for John's father. Jack Hinckley was a self-made millionaire, faithful Christian, regular churchgoer, and a devoted husband. Sud-denly, he became the bewildered father of an attempted assassin in the full glare of an inescapable national spotlight. Today the Hinckleys lead dramatically different lives.

Having moved from their comfortable Colorado home to be near their son, they live in a two-bedroom apartment with leased furniture in McLean, Virginia. They give much of their time and energy to the American Mental Health Fund, an organization they founded in 1985. They wish to publi-cize the warning signs of mental illness so other parents can spot what the Hinckleys failed to notice.

Hinckley says he would have enjoyed doing dozens of

other things at this time of life, but he knows in his heart he's doing the right thing. He made the decision to cause something good to come from John's illness. Hinckley can't think of anything more worthwhile than helping the mentally ill.

Leaving Philippi, Silas and Paul pushed to Thessalonica. 100 miles away, Thessalonica was the largest and most important city in Macedonia. Paul preached in the synagogue three Sabbaths. Some of the Jews believed, "as did a large number of God-fearing Greeks and not a few prominent women" (Acts 17:4, NIV).

Silas was a coworker of Paul's during the several months of ministry in Thessalonica. The two of them, with Timothy, worked hard to support themselves during their stay. Paul later wrote, "laboring night and day, because we would not be chargeable unto any of you" (1 Thes. 2:9). Silas did not loaf in their midst or take any free meals but rather supported himself so as not to be a burden to anyone.

In Thessalonica, as in every other city, opposition to the teaching of Paul and Silas sprang up. Jewish leaders aroused the rabble to attack the house of Jason, a convert with whom Paul and Silas were lodging. The two missionaries were out at the time, so Jason and other believers were dragged before the authorities who released them on receipt of money which would guarantee that these believers would uphold the peace. This meant Silas and Paul would get Jason into serious trouble and financial loss unless they left the city. Sadly, but wisely, they left (Acts 17:10). When Paul later wrote the Thessalonians two letters, each time he included Silas in the opening greetings, though using his Roman name of Silvanus (1 Thes. 1:1; 2 Thes. 1:1).

At Berea, about 40 miles southwest of Thessalonica, the Jews were more open-minded than in most places, readily discussing the Old Testament prophecies which Paul now declared as fulfilled in the Death and Resurrection of Christ. But when a delegation of Jewish leaders came to Berea and stirred up trouble, the believers sent Paul away to Athens. Paul left Silas and Timothy at Berea (Acts 17:14).

Though Silas was by Paul's side most of the second missionary journey, he remained behind after Paul's departure to carry on the work. Silas, a prophet, was undoubtedly a forceful and capable preacher and teacher of the Word. He certainly continued to help the Bereans search the Scriptures daily. He engaged in follow-up work, strengthening the converts. He was assisted by the younger member of the team, Timothy, who doubtless grew under Silas' tutelage. How wise is the modern soul-winner who makes sure new converts are enrolled in some systematic follow-up course or discipled by some mature Christian.

Silas and Timothy Join Paul in Corinth

Two hundred miles south of Berea lay Athens, the intellectual center of the ancient world, the city of Socrates, Plato, and Aristotle. After a short time here during which he gave an address on Mars Hill, Paul went on to Corinth, the political and commercial capital of Achaia and channel of trade between East and West. When Silas and Timothy joined him at Corinth, Paul devoted himself to the preaching of the Word, ministering for over a year and a half (Acts 18:11). When Paul left Corinth, again he seems to have left Silas behind. We have no further record of Silas in the company of Paul. Doubtless, for some time he was still a member of Paul's team filling assignments for the great Apostle elsewhere.

Silas was content to play second fiddle. It's never easy to take a subordinate position to a person of outstanding ability and strong personality. But one characteristic of a Christian servant is his readiness for inconspicuous service in places of secondary significance. Silas subjugated any ambition to command, content to follow the richly endowed Apostle as a loyal companion and team member.

7. Timothy, the Understudy

It was an unlikely combination! Paul was around 50 years of age. Timothy may still have been a teenager, perhaps 19.

Paul must have had an iron constitution to endure his rugged travels, frequent beatings, prolonged imprisonments, and countless privations. Timothy seemed frail of health, the recipient of a medical prescription to help his queasy stomach overcome its "frequent spells of illness" (1 Tim. 5:23, PH).

Paul was a born leader; Timothy was a willing follower. He-man Paul burned with zeal; timid Timothy needed frequent reminders to exert courage.

Despite their differences, Paul and Timothy developed a beautiful friendship. Timothy became Paul's dearest associate and indispensable traveling companion. Invited by Paul to join his traveling team, Timothy immediately left the pleasant home of his loving mother and grandmother to share the apostle's missionary labors and certain sufferings. This began a devoted fellowship with Timothy serving Paul "as a son with the father" (Phil. 2:22). They became one in joys and in sorrows.

With his warm fatherly heart Paul noted the spiritual growth of his son in the faith. Possessing no son of his own, perhaps Paul entertained the idea of adopting Timothy as his heir. He seems to have played a father's role in advising Timothy to submit to circumcision (Acts 16:3).

Paul regarded Timothy as his understudy. He trained his "son" to take his place when he was unable to minister. Paul aimed at reproducing himself in his youthful prodigy. He modeled sound doctrine, godly living, driving purpose, faith, patience in suffering and persecutions, and love (2 Tim. 3:10-11), so that Timothy could properly represent him (1 Cor. 4:17).

Not as forceful as Titus, tender and loyal Timothy met that need for understanding so often expressed in the apostle's writings. Someone suggested Timothy thought of himself as "the disciple Paul loved." On occasions of separation, Paul, yearning for the physical presence of his son in the faith, urged Timothy to hurry to his side. Though defects in Timothy's character are often inferred from instructions given him in the Pastoral Epistles, these inferences might be exaggerated in the light of Timothy's long and unswerving fidelity to Paul. Despite Timothy's appearance of weakness against the mountainous strength of Paul, he must have possessed sufficient force of character for Paul to expend such effort over his training and to find his company so essential They needed each other, the spiritual father and the beloved son. For 16 years their two hearts beat as one in the service of Christ, sharing joys and sorrows.

Timothy's Godly Heritage
Anatoly B. Shcharansky, Jewish activist who had been serving a 13-year sentence for alleged treason, espionage, and anti-Soviet agitation, was released from a Soviet labor camp

in February 1986 as part of an East-West prisoner exchange. When his guards tried to confiscate a book of Psalms his wife had sent him from Israel, Anatoly flung himself in the snow and refused to continue on his way. Speaking on Israeli television, he reported, "I said I would not leave the country without the Psalms which helped me so much. Not another step."

Over 19 centuries ago the Old Testament Scriptures also played a vital part in the life of Timothy. Paul wrote to him, "from a child thou hast known the holy Scriptures" (2 Tim. 3:15). Because Paul's first visit to Timothy's hometown of Lystra did not occur until Timothy was well into his teens, his training in the Scriptures obviously took place before he was converted. It's likely that both his teachers, his mother and grandmother, were won to Christ through Paul's ministry, so they were unsaved when they taught the lad Scripture. You can almost see his mother calling him in each night and faithfully reading him a portion of Scripture. The reading of the Old Testament prophecies prepared son, mother, and grandmother for the message of the Messiah, helping to make them wise unto salvation.

Timothy's mother, Eunice, and his grandmother, Lois, were both Jewesses, who doubtless took extra pains to rear him in the faith of his Jewish forefathers. Nothing is known of Timothy's father, except that he was a Gentile. Probably not a believer, he forbad Timothy's circumcision but didn't object to the name Eunice gave her son, which means "God-honoring," or to his Jewish training. Perhaps he had passed away before Paul's visit. How much the world owes to godly mothers like Eunice, Hannah, Elizabeth, and the Virgin Mary.

Grandmother Lois possessed a piety which impressed Paul. He wrote of the genuine faith which both she and mother Eunice possessed (2 Tim. 1:5). A German proverb says, "A grandmother's correction makes no impression."

But the training of this godly grandmother left its mark on Timothy's character. Incidentally, this is the only mention of the word *grandmother* in the Bible. *Grandfather* never occurs.

The story is told of a boy who was raised by parents who never darkened the door of a church. During his childhood, however, he spent several of his summers on the farm of godly grandparents who not only took him to church every Sunday, but also explained the Gospel to him at opportune times. In young adulthood, when he joined a Gospel-preaching church, he testified that it was the witness of his grandparents that led him to Christ.

Timothy's conversion. Paul's first missionary journey took him through cities of Asia Minor. When he and his team got wind of a plot on Iconium to stone them, they fled to Lystra and environs where "there they preached the gospel" (Acts 14:7). It was at this time that Timothy's family was converted, perhaps the women first, then Timothy. At Lystra, Paul also healed a crippled man, and he and Barnabas were acclaimed as gods. Later, the fickle crowd turned on Paul and stoned him, leaving him for dead outside the city gates. Teenage Timothy never could have forgotten that scene. No wonder Paul reminded him in later years, "Thou hast fully known my . . . persecutions, afflictions, which came unto me at Antioch, at Iconium, at Lystra; what persecutions I endured: but out of them all the Lord delivered me" (2 Tim. 3:10-11). How vividly Timothy must have recalled that, after the stoning of Paul, an apparently lifeless form began to stir suddenly out of the rubble of rocks. Then Paul rose and walked into the city.

Years earlier, as a young man, Paul had watched Stephen die by stoning, a scene that had etched itself on his memory in indelible conviction. Now, as Paul suffered a stoning, young Timothy also had a picture of a stoning etched on his mind. Tradition says that the wounded Paul stayed in the home of Eunice and Lois that night. How impressed Timothy must have been with the reality of Christ when Paul was so willing to suffer for Him. The next day when Paul left for Derbe, Timothy might have watched his form disappearing in the distance and wondered if he would ever see him again. But Paul did return.

His Call to Join Paul

Five or so years later, on a second visit to Lystra, Paul invited Timothy to join his team (Acts 16:1-3).

Why would Paul choose this lad? He was probably not yet 20, and in that culture only the elders received a respectful hearing. He came from a small, rural town with not enough Jews to have a synagogue. Timothy's education, though not deficient in the Scriptures, was certainly not of seminary standard. His health was frail. He possessed an inferiority complex. Maybe he was a mama's boy. The last time Paul had taken along a youth as an aide, that young man, Mark, had left for home. Why not pick someone else like Silas, and thus have two seasoned veterans instead of one veteran and one novice? Wouldn't this fearful boy run at the sight of the first stone?

Reasons for Paul's invitation. Timothy was highly regarded, not only by the Christians in his hometown of Lystra, but also by those in Iconium, 18 miles away (Acts 16:2). He impressed the area church leaders as an unusually dedicated young man, thus not without honor in his own country. He fulfilled the qualification of a minister which Paul later mentioned in a letter to Timothy, "He must also have a good reputation with outsiders" (1 Tim. 3:7, NIV). Timothy had already made a good beginning in an active ministry for Christ.

Paul constantly looked for workers to carry the Gospel.

Like Jesus as he observed the plenteous harvest, he lamented the paucity of laborers. Here was a promising young man who might help fill the demand.

Paul sensed the need for someone who could symbolize a combination of outreach to both Jews and Gentiles. Timothy, with his mother's Old Testament instruction and his upbringing in a Gentile culture, would fill the bill. Silas, as a Jerusalem Jew, didn't have the same appeal.

Timothy also represented a new generation. To guarantee perpetuity of Gospel preaching, discipling a person 30 years his junior was a good strategy. Also, many of the converts would be of a youthful age and might feel more at home with someone of their peer group teaching and encouraging them.

Perhaps Paul saw that Timothy needed a challenge bigger than a ministry around Lystra could give him. Though adding another staff member would create interpersonal problems, Paul weighed the pluses and the minuses and invited Timothy.

Timothy's circumcision. Paul knew that Gentiles would listen to Timothy preach, but Jews would not listen because of his uncircumcised condition. On the suggestion of Paul, Timothy, to his credit, submitted to the painful operation of circumcision. Paul seemed to leave himself open to the charge of inconsistency because in the case of Titus he had refused to circumcise him, but now in the case of Timothy he advocates the rite. If Paul had given in and circumcised Titus, the Gentile, the action would have been tantamount to saying that circumcision was essential for salvation. To that Paul would never agree. In fact, he and Silas had just come from the Jerusalem Council, carrying letters containing the Council's decree that salvation was by faith apart from circumcision. Though he knew how to fight for principle when necessary, as in Titus' instance, he also knew how to smooth out difficulties when no principle was at stake. Since Timothy's mother was a Jewess, his uncircumcised state would be perennially objectionable to a Jewish audience, so Paul was willing to acquiesce for the sake of expediency. Paul was willing to be made all things to all men to win some (1 Cor. 9:22).

His ordination. Timothy was called before the leaders and gave an excellent account of his faith. A solemn service of ordination was held in which he was dedicated to the ministry. Paul reminded Timothy of this occasion when he wrote, "Neglect not the gift that is in thee, which was given thee by prophecy, with the laying on of hands of the presbytery" (1 Tim. 4:14). Paul referred to his own part in that ordination service, "Wherefore I put thee in remembrance that thou stir up the gift of God, which is in thee by the putting on of my hands" (2 Tim. 1:6). Paul later reminded his understudy of "the prophecies once made about you" (1 Tim. 1:18, NIV).

How often do Christian workers, when the fire burns low, need to remind themselves of their early vows of consecration, renew their habits of study, and rekindle their devotion and zeal.

After that ordination service, Paul hovered over Timothy as a mother hen hovers over her chicks. Paul, however, esteemed Timothy a brother, a fellow worker, a fellow servant, and a fellow apostle (1 Thes. 3:2; Phil. 1:1; Rom. 16:21; 1 Thes. 1:1; 2:6). Although a minor apostle compared to Paul, Timothy nevertheless performed an important apostolic ministry.

His Many Years of Devoted Association with Paul

Timothy must have enjoyed making the rounds of Asia Minor cities, observing the delivery of the decrees from the Jerusalem Council and also seeing the various churches established in the faith and increasing in number daily (Acts 16:4-5). Seeing Paul get divine direction for a trip to Macedonia must also have been enlightening (Acts 16:6-10). Little did he know what awaited him at Philippi as he took what may well have been his first major boat ride, sailing from Troas to Neapolis. (His hometown of Lystra was 100 miles from the Mediterranean.)

With Paul in Philippi. Paul led a group of women to Christ and commanded an evil spirit to come out of a demon possessed girl. Then Paul and Silas found themselves severely beaten and jailed. Despite incarceration in the inner dungeon and bruised, bloody backs, they sang praises to God at midnight.

Timothy and Luke, for some reason, were not imprisoned. They were probably praying in the home of Lydia, a wealthy merchant who had become the first convert at Philippi, and who had opened her home to Paul and his team. Other recent believers had come to join them in prayer. The next morning Paul and Silas, released by the magistrates who by now realized their mistake in beating Roman citizens, went to Lydia's home and encouraged the believers (Acts 16:40). Wouldn't you think that instead of Paul encouraging others, others would be encouraging him? Profound must have been the effect of Paul's account of the earthquake and the conversion of the Philippian jailer on this stripling, Timothy, maybe still in his teens. For the first time, he shared in the planting of a new church. He learned from Paul's experience that God could transform tribulation into triumph. But he must have wondered, *If I were tossed into jail unjustly, would I be able to sing at high noon, let alone at dark midnight? Or would I sulk?* His training had begun.

In Thessalonica. Luke stayed behind in Philippi to stabilize the infant church. Some think Timothy stayed too, but others believe he joined Paul and Silas who, forced to leave, trudged down Via Egnata, the main road to Thessalonica, a 100-mile, 3-day walk, to a city with a population of 200,000. At Philippi, Timothy had seen how a church could be started in a Gentile city. Now he was to participate in planting a church in a city with a large Jewish population. Paul followed his typical approach of visiting the synagogue on the Sabbath and showing from the Scriptures that the Messiah would suffer and rise from the dead. Then he would declare that this Jesus whom he preached was the fulfillment of those prophecies, and thus the promised Messiah (Acts 17:3).

To earn their bread, the three of them worked during the week (1 Thes. 2:9). Timothy and Silas joined Paul in his tentmaking trade or engaged in other crafts. Timothy saw how tentmaking and synagogue evangelism combined to produce a host of new converts.

The smooth road soon turned rough. A rowdy mob, encouraged by the synagogue leaders, stormed the home of Jason where Paul, Silas, and perhaps Timothy were living, but who, providentially, were out at the moment. The mob dragged Jason to court, charging him and the absent missionaries with subversive conduct. Timothy, who had seen Paul stoned at Lystra and beaten and jailed at Philippi, must have wondered if this time it might be his own turn to suffer. But his fears were allayed when he learned that the town fathers were only demanding Jason's guarantee that the missionaries would leave and cause no more commotion. That night, after a stay of three or so months, the missionaries left for Berea, 50 miles away, where they planted a Bible-loving church. The jealous leaders at Thessalonica, however, made a trip to Berea to stir up the people there against the missionaries, so the believers sent Paul to Athens while Timothy and Silas stayed at Berea. But soon Paul sent for Timothy to join him at Athens (Acts 17:10-15).

At this time Timothy received his first solo assignment. He had been with Paul just a year or so and would have been only 20 or 21, not quite the age at which many students begin seminary today. Paul sent Timothy back to Thessalonica, the scene of much opposition to the Gospel, to stabilize the people in their newfound faith. Paul explained in a letter:

So when we could stand it no longer, we thought it best to be left by ourselves in Athens. We sent Timothy, who is our brother and God's fellow worker in spreading the gospel of Christ, to strengthen and encourage you in your faith, so that no one would be unsettled by these trials (1 Thes. 3:1-3, NIV).

Happily, his mission was successful. He returned to Paul later with tidings of the faith of the Thessalonians, their love, and their fond memories of Paul. This report brought comfort to Paul. In ensuing years Timothy would travel on many more similar assignments as a stand-in for the Apostle, encouraging, warning, teaching, reminding, and supporting, in a ministry author William Petersen calls "shuttle diplomacy."

Commentator William Barclay states:

One of the special things about Timothy is that time and time again we read about Paul sending him somewhere. In fact, Timothy must have spent most of his life going on expeditions on which Paul sent him.

Barclay compares Timothy to a postage stamp:

The postage stamp sticks to its job. It is stuck on the envelope and there it stays until it has reached its destination. The person who lets the difficulties beat him never arrives anywhere. A good messenger never gives up until he has delivered his message. Second, the postage stamp goes where it is sent. Stick it on the envelope and it will go to Edinburgh, or London, to Paris, or Berlin, to Peking, or Timbuctoo. . . . It did not matter to Timothy where he was sent. He went. It was enough for him that Paul wanted him to go. . . . One of the great tests of any person is if he can really put his back into things that he does not want to do (*God's Young Church*, Westminster, p. 105).

Timothy, Paul's understudy, had passed a major test as a trainee in his visit to Thessalonica.

In Corinth. Paul left Athens and proceeded to Corinth, a commercial, cosmopolitan crossroad, of half a million people. There Timothy and Silas joined him in what was to be a year and a half of successful church building. Because Paul mentioned that he baptized very few of the Corinthian converts, many believe Timothy and Silas performed most of the baptisms. From Corinth, Paul wrote his Epistle to the Romans in which he sent a greeting from "Timothy my fellow worker" (Rom. 16:21). Timothy stayed with Paul through the end of the second missionary journey and through the start of the third journey until they reached Ephesus.

While at Ephesus, they learned of serious problems at Corinth. After unsuccessful communication with the church at Corinth, Paul finally sent Timothy back to straighten out the situation. He told the Corinthians, "For this cause I sent unto you Timotheus, who is my beloved son, and faithful in the Lord, who shall bring you into remembrance of my ways which be in Christ, as I teach everywhere in every church" (1 Cor. 4:17). He endorsed Timothy as his personal representative and as the Lord's worker and told them not to despise this young man (1 Cor. 16:10-11). Though Paul tried to pave the way for Timothy's visit, the Corinthians didn't heed his advice. Probably the problems were overwhelming, involving both doctrine and morals, complicated by four church divisions, and practicing legalists, libertines, philosophers, and mystics. Though capable and godly, Timothy failed simply because of lack of experience. He seemed too young. Why hadn't Paul come in person? Paul may not have realized the enormity of the situation or he wouldn't have pushed Timothy in over his depth.

After hearing the news from Timothy, making a quick trip, and writing another letter, Paul dispatched Titus, the troubleshooter, who brought back a good report to Paul. Out of joy Paul wrote what is known as 2 Corinthians. He began the letter, "Paul . . . and Timothy," showing that Timothy's failure didn't reduce his status one iota. Soon Paul and Timothy would visit Corinth again. Perhaps Timothy would be somewhat embarrassed to meet those who had previously mistreated him. And he had to learn to forgive them, as had Paul. This entire experience with the Corinthian church was also part of Timothy's apprenticeship as Paul's understudy.

In Rome. The last mention of Timothy in Acts finds him at Troas with the delegation commissioned to carry an offering from the Gentile churches to the needy Jewish believers at Jerusalem (Acts 20:4). Though we assume Timothy was also with Paul on his final Jerusalem visit and during some of his two-year detention at Caesarea, we lose track of him until we find him in Rome during Paul's first imprisonment. Writing from his own hired house, Paul included Timothy in the salutation of three of his Prison Epistles (Phil. 1:1; Col. 1:1; Philemon 1:1).

Expecting to be released from Rome soon, Paul told the Philippians he hoped to send Timothy to them before long.

Barnabas had traveled with Paul on only one journey, as had Silas, but Timothy was still with Paul. Timothy was faithful. Without genius, he was not without goodness. Paul wrote:

> But I trust . . . to send Timotheus shortly unto you. . . . For I have no man likeminded, who will naturally care for your state. For all seek their own, not the things which are Jesus Christ's. But ye know the proof of him, that, as a son with the father, he hath served with me in the gospel (Phil. 2:19-22).

The context of this Philippian passage deals with the mind-set of Christ which led Him to surrender the comforts of heaven to suffer the cross of Calvary on our behalf. Timothy was an outstanding example of the mind of Christ, being willing to inconvenience himself on behalf of the Philippians. Not a soul at Rome was sufficiently disinterested in self to do what Timothy was going to do. Love of family, ease, and comfort made them unwilling to sacrifice their own quiet security. To Paul this indicated they hadn't yet learned Christlikeness. Had Christ taken the same attitude, He would have remained in the ivory palaces, and we would have remained in our sins. Those who seek their own affairs do not follow Christ's example.

Before we're too hard on these self-seeking Christians though, let's take an inventory and note how often we fail to give up our comforts and plans to do the Lord's bidding. Many Christians prefer the ease of an armchair in front of the TV over an hour at the prayer meeting or an evening of visitation for the church.

The Pastoral Epistles Addressed to Timothy
Again there's a gap in the record. If Timothy ever reached Philippi, we're not told. The next time we hear of Timothy,

he is at Ephesus where Paul has joined him. Then Paul left and asked Timothy to stay at Ephesus (1 Tim. 1:3). One day Timothy received a letter (1 Timothy), then later he received another (2 Timothy). Timothy needed these letters. After at least 13 years in the apostle's constant company, except for a few assignments and separations caused by Paul's arrests, Timothy now had a long-term task to do alone. The church in Ephesus, one of the five largest cities in the Roman Empire, was quite a challenge. Still considered a youth at 33, with a seemingly timid disposition and a queasy stomach, he needed all the encouragement he could get. In these letters Paul encouraged him to be:

- a faithful minister of the truth
- an opponent of false teachers
- an encourager of public prayer and qualified church officers
- an example in manner of life, word, and purity
- a pastor to all age groups and social classes
- an admonisher of the rich
- a good and fearless soldier of Jesus Christ.

Some scholars suggest that Timothy, away from Paul's overshadowing presence, may have eased up a bit and so needed a warning against youthful lusts, love of money, and laxity in the use of his gift. Was not Paul merely behaving like any father as he contemplated a son facing the wiles of the world? After all, Paul's high esteem of Timothy was shown by calling him a "man of God" (1 Tim. 6:11). Paul also craved the company of Timothy in the dark and difficult hours of his final imprisonment.

Summoned to Rome
In prison for the final time, no longer in his own hired house but in the dreaded, damp Mamertine dungeon, Paul sensed his imminent martyrdom. He could say, "I have

fought a good fight, I have finished my course, I have kept the faith" (2 Tim. 4:7). He had no fear of death for he knew that to die was gain. But he missed his friends, so he wanted Timothy to come before the cold of winter. He had already dispatched Tychicus to temporarily replace Timothy as pastor at Ephesus. Timothy was to bring Mark, a warm cloak, books, and parchments (2 Tim. 4:9-13). For the comfort of Timothy's affection, Paul was willing to ask him to travel 1,000 miles. In no time Timothy packed his bags and was on his way.

Whether the two ever saw each other again is not recorded. It may be that on the way to see Paul, Timothy paid the penalty for his bravery by getting thrown into jail himself. This might explain the reference to Timothy's imprisonment in Hebrews 13:23, "Know ye that our brother Timothy is set at liberty." (Incidentally, Timothy is the only living person mentioned in Hebrews.)

We can hope that Paul had the comfort of Timothy's company, as well as that of Mark, Luke, and others when the end came. What a privilege to walk with Paul to the place of his execution outside of Rome. Timothy was true to the very end.

The Timothy Principle
The Navigators have coined the expression, "the Timothy principle." The principle states that God's basic plan for perpetuating life, both physical and spiritual, is through reproduction. Only life reproduces life. Each believer is an instrument through which the Gospel flows to another person to give him eternal life; thus believers bring forth fruit. The principle is based on 2 Timothy 2:2 where Timothy is exhorted to pass on the truth he received from Paul to the faithful men who in turn will teach others.

In his book *Presenting Belief in An Age of Unbelief,*

Chuck Colson says:

> Our task is not simply to get people to recite certain
> prayers so we can move on to more fertile fields. We are
> to help lead them to Christ and then teach them spiritual
> disciplines and truths so that they truly can become disci-
> ples—followers of Christ, and in time teachers them-
> selves. . . . When I asked Christ into my life, I had never
> heard of evangelical Christianity. . . . If there hadn't been
> someone to take me by the hand and walk me through
> the Scriptures, help me to pray, help me feel comfortable
> with others, I really wonder where I would be today.
> Doug Coe discipled me constantly. Harold Hughes, my
> one time political enemy, loved me even when most peo-
> ple in my own political party turned their back on me. Al
> Quie, then a Congressman, offered to go to prison for me.
> Fred Rhodes took an early retirement from government
> to help me start my ministry. And down through the
> years there have been men like Carl Henry, Richard Love-
> lace, R.C. Sproul, Dick Halverson, and others who have
> given so much of themselves to teach me. Whatever
> growth I have experienced as a Christian has been in
> large measure due to the sacrificial commitment of others
> who were willing to invest themselves in me" (Victor,
> pp. 29-31).

When Timothy was released from prison, that wasn't the
end of his service. However timid he may have been, he was
not a quitter. He came back to face whatever was in store
for him. According to tradition, Timothy was martyred in
Ephesus about 20 years later, during the reign of Emperor
Domitian.

Like father, like son!

8. Luke, the Physician

In the city of Ferkessedougou in northern Ivory Coast, Africa, at the 60 bed Conservative Baptist Mission Hospital, doctors and nurses see more than 12,000 new patients every year. Altogether, a total of 45,000 patients come annually for medical care, 2,000 of them as inpatients, 600 of whom have major medical or surgical problems. The staff has to limit clinic visits to 150 per day to handle the press of emergencies.

Privileged to visit this 14 acre property in the fall of 1986, my wife and I witnessed an emergency cesarean section. A mother, already in labor for 24 hours and unable to deliver, had been rushed by taxi over rough roads from a government hospital 60 miles away. The baby was successfully delivered by Dr. John Slater. Without the mission hospital, both baby and mother would likely have died. John and his brother, Dr. Dwight Slater, are in charge of this 25-year-old, highly regarded medical complex to which 10 regional government hospitals refer complicated cases.

The brothers regard their medical work as a threefold

ministry. First, medicine is considered as a means of evangelism. Hundreds have found Christ through the medical ministry of this hospital. Patients, families, and friends are invited to regularly conducted services held on the hospital's veranda. Personal witness is given along with patient care. An old Vietnamese man, treated by the hospital, helped start a new church. Each week teams, including the doctors, go out from the hospital to teach Bible classes in the public schools and to conduct Sunday services in outlying villages.

Second, the hospital provides medical care for believers, especially new converts who need somewhere to go when they turn their backs on the witch doctors with their sorcerous cures.

Third, the hospital tries to care for the physical ills of Christian workers of various denominations. Missionary families from considerable distances come to occupy guest houses a few weeks before a baby's expected arrival. The hospital wants to keep the Christian troops at the front of the battle.

The Slater brothers are not the first to combine medicine and evangelism. Granddaddy of all medical missionaries was Dr. Luke. Not only did he accompany Paul on many of his travels as his personal physician, but he also was left behind at Philippi as a spiritual pediatrician to tend to the growing pains of an infant church. In addition, he authored two of the first five New Testament books, the Gospel of Luke and the history of Acts. The abrupt and seemingly unfinished ending of Acts has led many Bible scholars to conclude that Luke had intended to write a third book.

Luke, the Doctor
Would a doctor of the first century have had much medical knowledge? Would we want someone to perform surgery on us today who had only the training possessed by Luke?

Medical texts before 1700 B.C. do not deserve to be called scientific because they are a mixture of home remedies, herb cures, incantations, and astute observations on body functions. Through following centuries medical information grew to a limited degree. But between the sixth century B.C. and the second century A.D. medicine achieved advances greater than at any other period in history, except the last two centuries.

What boosted medical knowledge was the rise of science in the sixth century B.C., largely due to the Greek method of abstracting principles from empirical data through observing, comparing, and deducing. William S. LaSor says that this method was well-known, particularly in the medical field so "Luke was heir to a science of medicine that could compare favorably with any medical practice up to the early part of the last century" (*Great Personalities of the New Testament*, Revell, p. 130). Luke was no medical ignoramus.

F.L. Godet in his *Commentary on the Gospel of Luke* wrote:

> There existed at Rome, in the time of the Emperors, a medical supervision; a superior college (Collegium archiatrorum) was charged with the duty of examining in every city those who desired to practice the healing art. Newly admitted men were placed under the direction of old physicians; their modes of treatment were strictly scrutinized, and their mistakes severely punished, sometimes by taking away their diploma. For these reasons, Luke must have possessed an amount of scientific and literary culture above that of most of the other evangelists and apostles" (Kregel, p.11).

This accounts for his use of technical medical terminology.
His Belief in the Virgin Birth. The account of the Virgin

Birth of Jesus occurs in two Gospels. How significant that one of those accounts was written by a physician. With unmistakable plainness Luke relates that Mary, apart from cohabitation with a man, became the mother of Jesus. The story is factual, related as history by none less than a doctor whose medical knowledge equaled that of a physician who practiced at the start of the last century (Luke 1:26-56).

A blatant infidel once challenged a Christian physician on his belief in the Virgin Birth of Jesus, asking cynically, "Suppose an attractive young woman came to you and told you that she was with child by the Holy Ghost. Would you believe her?"

The physician calmly replied, "Probably not. I would be suspicious if some ordinary woman came to me with such a statement. But if the child was born and grew into a miraculous man, demonstrating a supernatural character and power, healing the sick, cleansing the leper, changing water into wine, raising the dead, teaching as no other man taught, then rose to life after being three days dead, I would be forced to reevaluate my attitude toward the woman's claims and conclude she could easily have had a miraculous conception of that child."

Luke, who had researched the facts of Jesus' supernatural deeds, His incomparable teaching, His sinless life, the infallible proofs of His resurrection (Acts 1:3), and His ascension into heaven, had no trouble accepting the Virgin Birth, even as a physician.

His interest in healing. Besides relating most of the miracles recorded in the other Gospels, Luke is the only one to relate the healing of the woman crippled 18 years (13:10-13), the healing of the man with dropsy (14:1-6), the cleansing of the ten lepers (17:11-19), and the healing of the high priest's servant's ear, cut off at Jesus' arrest (22:50-51). Luke also records physical phenomena such as Jesus sweating drops of blood (22:44) and eating food in the upper room in His resurrected body (24:42-43).

In Acts, Luke records the healing of the lame man at the temple gate (3:1-8), the healing of Aeneas (9:33-34), the healing of the cripple at Lystra (14:8-10), the miraculous raising of Paul after a stoning when his followers thought him dead (14:19-20), the resuscitation of Eutychus at Troas (20:9-12), the failure of a viper's poisonous bite to kill Paul on Malta (28:1-6), and the curing of Publius' father, also on Malta (28:7-10).

The tenderness of Dr. Luke shows in his references to *only* children. The raising from the dead of the young man of Nain contains the human interest element that he was the *only* son of his widowed mother. Jesus had compassion on her and delivered this *only* son back to his mother (Luke 7:11-15). Luke records two other miracles in which the *only* daughter of Jairus is raised from the dead (8:41-42), and a demented boy, the *only* son of his father, is healed (9:38-40). Though these two miracles are related in other Gospels, Luke alone uses the word *only*.

Luke, the Companion

A man in his 70s planned an overseas trip. Not in the best of health because of his heart, he was delighted to learn that a doctor, a cardiologist at that, would be in his travel group.

Paul had his own personal physician from the middle of his second missionary journey to the end of his life. Some scholars think Luke was born in Syrian Antioch; others that he came from Philippi and was "the man of Macedonia" in Paul's Troas night vision (Acts 16:9). Because of his seeming familiarity with the sea and ships, some believe Luke was once a ship's doctor. Additional conjecture suggests that Paul's "thorn in the flesh" was a physical affliction which required the attention of a doctor so that Luke was called in to treat him. At any rate, Luke, already a believer, joined Paul's team at Troas which included Silas and Timothy. The use of the pronoun *they* (Acts 16:4, 6-8) gives way to the pronouns *we* and *us* (Acts 16:10-16) indicating that Luke has joined the team.

After the use of *we* and *us* in Acts 16:10-16, a section which deals with the Philippian episode, these first person pronouns are not found again until Acts 20:5. The inference is that Luke was left at Philippi to strengthen the nucleus of new converts while Paul proceeded to other cities to evangelize. When Paul returned to Philippi on his third missionary journey, he picked up Luke, who from then on, became the apostle's almost constant companion, even on his final visit to Jerusalem and on the shipwrecked Mediterranean voyage to Rome.

Even a casual reading of Acts reveals that from chapter 20 to the end of the book, the travel route of Paul to Jerusalem, his beating outside the temple, his defense before the Sanhedrin, and his three trials at Caesarea are recorded with greater detail than any other part of the history. This was possible because Luke was with Paul, thus an eyewitness to all that transpired.

Luke accompanied Paul the prisoner on his stormy voyage to Italy, as did Aristarchus. Even a man's wife was not permitted to accompany a prisoner; so perhaps the two men passed as Paul's slaves, or Luke as his doctor.

Luke remained close to Paul until the end. During his incarceration in the awful Mamertine prison, with others on assignments, and Demas having forsaken him, Paul wrote, "Only Luke is with me" (2 Tim. 4:11). The loyal physician had followed Paul from Philippi to Troas to Jerusalem to Caesarea to Rome, all the while ministering to the apostle's physical needs.

God does use doctors, even though all healing comes

ultimately from Him. At times God used Paul to bring miraculous healing; on other occasions Paul apparently could not effect a miracle, as in the case of Epaphroditus when sick nigh unto death (Phil. 2:25-27). Nor could Paul cure his own thorn in the flesh.

Paul needed a doctor. If his thorn in the flesh was physical, like an eye problem, Luke was there to help. Paul had been whipped with 39 stripes by the Jews on five occasions, beaten three times by the cruel Roman lictors. He endured weariness, hunger, and thirst, suffering in cold and nakedness. He was frequently imprisoned and often exposed to death (2 Cor. 11:23-27). Through it all he had the solicitous and tender care of a competent physician. Perhaps his friends early in his ministry had seen the need and insisted that he should always have a doctor in attendance.

Luke, the Historian

Careful research. Luke, a well-educated man, was a laborious and conscientious researcher as well as a skillful writer. The *we* and *us* sections in Acts (16:10-17; 20:5–21:25; 27:2–28:16) are autobiographical. As we read, we feel as though we are looking over Luke's shoulder, becoming eyewitnesses along with him. But what about the rest of his writings, especially his biography of Jesus whom he had probably never seen, and whose follower he was certainly not known to be?

In the introduction to his Gospel, Luke seems to imply a sense of deficiency in the previously written accounts of Jesus' ministry, even though these accounts were penned by eyewitnesses and ministers. He wrote, "Many have undertaken to draw up an account of the things that have been fulfilled among us, just as they were handed down to us by those who from the first were eyewitnesses and servants of the word" (1:1-2, NIV). To give a more comprehensive and orderly account, he set about the task of firsthand investigation.

He made several journeys and conducted numerous interviews, sparing neither time nor money in the pursuit of accurate and hitherto unrecorded data on the Saviour's story. Those who had seen or heard Jesus on earth were becoming fewer, as death thinned their ranks. With not much time to spare, he set out to interview those of the Master's surviving family and followers who could supply significant insights. Not until then did he sit down and write: "Since I myself have carefully investigated everything from the beginning, it seemed good also to me to write an orderly account for you, most excellent Theophilus, so that you may know the certainty of the things you have been taught" (1:3-4, NIV). Theophilus was probably a Roman official whom Luke held in high respect.

Interestingly, Luke dedicated his second book, Acts, to the same person, "In my former book, Theophilus, I wrote about all that Jesus began to do and to teach until the day He was taken up to heaven" (Acts 1:1, NIV). The Gospel of Luke deals with Jesus' earthly ministry while Acts relates His ministry after the Ascension as He continued to work by His Holy Spirit through the Apostles.

Some who hold a narrow view of inspiration think it dishonoring to the Holy Spirit to speak of relying on any source except the Holy Spirit. But the traditional view of inspiration holds that the Holy Spirit inspired the authors in their use of sources, as well as in the words they employed.

The Virgin Mary was one of Luke's important sources. She opened her heart to Paul's personal physician and appointed researcher. She recounted to Luke conversations known only to God, Gabriel, Joseph, Jesus, and herself. Only in Luke do we have the record of the angel's appearance to Zacharias with the announcement of the birth of John the Baptist,

Gabriel's annunciation to Mary of the Virgin Birth of Jesus, Mary's visit to cousin Elizabeth, Mary's Magnificat, and the birth of John the Baptist. He also records the birth and circumcision of Jesus, the adoration of the shepherds and Simeon and Anna, and Jesus confounding the learned temple teachers at the age of 12.

Paul himself was Luke's major source. From Paul, Luke would have learned the details of Stephen's stoning, the apostle's Damascus road conversion, the ministry at Antioch and on the first missionary journey, the sharp difference with Barnabas, and the resultant separation. Luke also learned of those matters involving Paul when Luke was not personally present. Luke likely completed his research during Paul's two-year detention at Caesarea. Since Philip, the evangelist, lived in Caesarea, Luke easily gathered material from him. He could have traveled down to Jerusalem to talk to James, the brother of Jesus. Surely Silas, Mark, and Timothy also filled in facts where needed.

Historical Accuracy. Luke alone gives data which links the biblical story to the secular world. His careful research amassed an amazing amount of material. According to scholar R.C.H. Lenski 110 persons are named in Acts. Places, geographical details, titles, and local color are found on many pages. (*Interpretation of the Acts of the Apostles,* Wartburg Press, p. 5). At first, scholars tended to question Luke's historical credibility, citing supposed errors of fact. But in 1880 a classics scholar, Sir William Ramsay, made his first visit to Asia Minor to begin research that continued through the next 30 years. As he discovered detail after detail, he came to realize that Luke was a premier historian.

Ramsay asserted, "Every person is found just where he ought to be: proconsuls in senatorial provinces, asiarchs in Ephesus, strategoi in Philippi, politarchs in Thessalonica, magicians and soothsayers everywhere" (*The Bearing of*

Recent Discovery on the Trustworthiness of the New Testament, Hodder and Stoughton, pp. 96-97).

Ramsay, top-rated scholar in the field of Asia Minor's historical geography, found no defects in Luke's history. His many volumes have convinced not a few skeptical scholars as to Luke's remarkable accuracy as a trained historian.

Luke, the Gospeler

Luke wrote the third and longest of the four Gospels, reflecting the results of his painstaking research. But he wrote Luke and Acts, not merely for the sake of writing, but rather to present the "old, old story of Jesus and His Love" in a clear and convincing way to noble Theophilus and beyond to a wider circle of readers. Luke was an evangelist at heart. He wanted to herald the Gospel, which simply means "good news."

Emphasized salvation. Only Luke's Gospel contains the parables of the lost coin, the lost sheep, and the prodigal son (15:1-32). Only Luke's Gospel carries the story of Zaccheus, Jericho's rich but crooked tax collector who repented and heard Jesus say, "This day is salvation come to this house. . . . For the Son of man is come to seek and to save that which was lost" (19:9-10). Only Luke records the conversion of the dying thief (23:39-43). More than once Jesus is termed the Friend of sinners (7:34; 15:2; 19:7).

Likewise, the book of Acts stresses salvation from start to finish. On the Day of Pentecost, Peter preached the Good News of remission of sin through Jesus Christ's death and resurrection, resulting in the salvation of 3,000.

Luke also writes of several others who spread the Gospel. Stephen served tables and preached the Gospel to the Sanhedrin. Scattered by the persecution following Stephen's stoning, the saints went everywhere preaching the Good News. Saul, persecutor of the church, suddenly converted on the Damascus road, immediately began to preach the Gospel. Peter preached the joyful message of forgiveness to Cornelius' household. Paul and Barnabas were commissioned by the church of Antioch to carry the Good News to distant places. The Philippian jailer heard Paul exclaim, "Believe on the Lord Jesus Christ, and thou shalt be saved" (16:31).

Wrote about women and home life. Only Luke's Gospel records the birth stories involving mothers Elizabeth and Mary (1:5–2:52). He alone mentions the widow of Nain (7:11-17), the sinful woman who washed Jesus' feet with her tears (7:36-50), the women who supported Him financially (8:1-3), and the episode of Mary sitting at Jesus' feet while Martha busily prepared the meal (10:38-42).

Luke recounts the popularity of Jesus as a dinner guest in Matthew's home (5:29), and in Pharisees' houses (7:36; 11:37; 14:1). Jesus invited Himself to dine at Zaccheus' place (19:5). Luke also explains that after the Resurrection Jesus visited the Emmaus home and the upper room, eating in both spots (24:30, 42-43).

Wrote for Everybody. Luke's is a Gospel of universality. No narrow prejudice excludes any class. Expressing hope and sympathy to the poor and lowly, Luke warns against the perils of wealth. He alone records the parables of the rich fool (12:16-21) and of the rich man who in eternity begged for a drop of water from the poor beggar Lazarus (16:19-31). With Mark, Luke reports the poor widow's offering of two mites which in divine estimation exceeded the total gifts of all the rich men combined (21:1-4).

Luke records Simeon's prediction that Jesus will be a "light to the Gentiles" (2:32), and that repentance and remission of sins will be preached among all nations (24:47).

Expressed joy. A quick scan of Acts highlights a jubilant and triumphant people. Early believers ate their meat with gladness (2:46-47). The lame man was healed and entered the temple, leaping and praising God (3:9). Philip's preaching in Samaria brought great joy to the city (8:8). The newly converted and baptized Ethiopian goes on his way rejoicing. Persecutor Saul is transformed into an apostle. If we follow Paul from prison to prison, from privation to privation, we find him glorying in tribulation, rejoicing in sorrow, and singing praises at midnight in jail.

This emphasis on joy in Acts is not surprising, for Luke began his Gospel with the songs of Mary, Zacharias, and the angels and ended it with the joyful thanksgiving of the disciples (24:52-53), items omitted by Matthew, Mark, and John.

Following Luke's footsteps. Through the years many doctors, like Dr. Walter Wilson, Dr. M.R. DeHaan, and Dr. Martyn Lloyd-Jones, have heard the call of God to give up their practices and devote all their time to the ministry of the Word. The majority of Christian doctors, however, combine scientific training and evangelistic passion, quietly praying and witnessing as they go about their daily practice. Interestingly, a group of clergy and laity from many backgrounds who feel compelled to make the ministry of healing a regular part of their vocation have organized under the name, Order of St. Luke.

Many doctors following in the footsteps of Luke have become medical missionaries. One such medical missionary is Dr. John Slater, a Conservative Baptist medical doctor serving in the Ivory Coast. Dr. Slater finds inspiration in words of David Livingstone, a missionary to Africa in the 1800s:

"God's only Son was a physician and a missionary,
A poor, poor imitation am I, or ever hope to be.
But in this service I wish to live,
And in it I hope to die."

9. Aquila and Priscilla, the Tutors

Gladys Aylward, a parlor maid, born in England in 1902 was convinced that God wanted her to be a missionary in China. Turned down by the China Inland Mission, she began saving every penny of her scant earnings to make deposits with the ticket agent at the railway station, the cheapest way to the Orient. Trying to learn everything possible about China, she corresponded with a widowed missionary who needed someone to come out and help her.

With her ticket fully paid, Gladys Aylward took a train out of the Liverpool station in 1932. Carrying a bedroll, two suitcases (one stocked with food), and a bag clanking with a small stove and pots and pans, she looked more like a vagabond than a missionary. At first the trip was uneventful, but in Russia, she found herself in the midst of an undeclared border war with China, the only woman aboard the train. When the train ground to a halt amid the sound of gunfire, yards from the war zone and unloaded hundreds of Russian soldiers and supplies, she had to climb off and begin trudging through the stark, Siberian landscape.

With a frigid wind blowing snow at her heels and still carrying all her baggage, this lonely figure shuffled through most of the night, silhouetted against the somber mountains and the black, star-studded sky. Oblivious to wolves in the area, she took a two-hour rest next to her petite cooking stove. She reached a railroad town the next day and took a train to Manchuria. But the only way she could get into China was by an unscheduled trip to Japan where she secured assistance from the British Consul.

Once in China, she had to trek across mountains to reach the missionary she came to help. Her first assignment involved operating an inn for muleteers passing through. The missionary gave these travelers the Gospel, while the girl from England did work far harder than the job she had left. But dealing with the muleteers enabled her to pick up the language. When the missionary died, Gladys was asked by the local magistrate to become the local foot inspector which required house-to-house enforcement of the laws against female footbinding. When war came, she took in abandoned children, adopting dozens of war orphans who depended on her for sustenance. After a breakdown in health and a slow recovery, she became employed by a local church to serve in evangelism and charity work.

In 1949, after 17 years in China, she finally made a visit home where she won the hearts of the British. She returned to make her home in Taiwan. A popular biography, *The Small Woman*, and a film on her story, *The Inn of Six Happinesses*, made her an international celebrity. Gladys Aylward had become one of the best known women missionaries of all time (Ruth A. Tucker, *From Jerusalem to Irian Jaya*, Zondervan, pp. 249-254).

By the mid-20th century the vital place of women in missions was well established. But even back in the first century women served as the Lord's servants in Christian ministry.

For example, a wife named Priscilla is mentioned along with her husband, Aquila, as fellow workers of Paul in his missionary labors. In fact, though they are always mentioned together, four of the six times Priscilla's name appears before Aquila's (Acts 18:2, 18, 26; Rom. 16:3; 1 Cor. 16:19; 2 Tim. 4:19). The precedence of her name over his may indicate higher social status as a member of a leading Roman family. Or it may highlight her more active Christian role and influence. Perhaps she outshone her husband in faith and deeds.

They Were Tentmakers

Aquila and Priscilla were forced to leave Rome by Emperor Claudius in A.D. 50. Aquila, a Jew whose family came from Pontus in northern Asia Minor, had been living with his wife at Rome when the order to expel Jews was issued. Their travels brought them to Corinth, where they settled, in early A.D. 51. Paul's arrival in Corinth on his second missionary journey occurred about this time.

Because Jewish parents made sure their children learned a trade, both Priscilla and Aquila had acquired the tentmaking occupation. This policy was supported by the Jewish proverb, "He that doesn't see to it that his son learns a trade teaches him to be a thief." As Paul was also a tentmaker, their mutual occupation soon brought them all together. Tents were made by weaving goat's hair cloth. This material was known as cilicium, owing to its connection with Cilicia, either as a point of origin or chief place of industry.

In America we do not usually concentrate all stores that sell identical items in the same district. But on a recent trip to Africa my wife and I noted how stores involved in the same commodity were often concentrated on the same street. We saw basketweavers, silversmiths, and dressmakers with their shops next to similar shops, happily directing a customer to a fellow craftsman for a rare or more pleasing article. It was the same in the first-century Near East. In Corinth Paul found his way to the street where the tentmakers plied their trade and met Priscilla and Aquila. Because nothing is said about any part Paul played in their conversion, it seems they had already been believers at Rome. The three of them soon discovered their common faith. Right away the couple invited Paul to stay with them. Together they worked at their business day after day. When Silas and Timothy arrived in Corinth, they too were likely invited to stay at the Priscilla-Aquila home, just as Lydia in Philippi had invited Paul's party of four to stay at her home.

What a blessed partnership as they lived and worked together. How they talked of the things of God as they made tents! When a person earns his living by a craft which has become automatic, his mind is free to think on other matters. Paul, Priscilla, and Aquila undoubtedly conversed on spiritual topics while goatskins under their skillful fingers turned into useful tents. They must have covered quite a theological curriculum together. How many questions the couple asked as they devoted themselves to acquiring spiritual knowledge! And what unforgettable answers from Paul! Intently they listened to Paul's Sabbath sermons in the synagogue. Already experts in tent making, they became proficient in Christian service, learning not only the tenets of the faith but also the skill of evangelization.

So capable was Priscilla that she was able to manage her considerable household duties and her tent-making occupation as well as study in the Word and assist Paul in the budding church at Corinth. Paul lived with this couple for about two years, training his coworkers with care and forming a close friendship that stretched through the next 17 or so years.

Tentmaker has become a technical word in missionary

language. It refers to a person who goes abroad to participate in missionary work but earns his livelihood through a
job, perhaps as a teacher, dentist, doctor, government official, or social worker. Some may not even have a formal
connection with any mission agency or may pay their own
passage to a mission field for a short term of service.

When the mission that sent William Carey, the father of
modern missions, failed to maintain his support in India, he
became a tentmaker, a foreman in an indigo factory. During
our country's early days, many preachers supported themselves by teaching school while their main purpose was to
evangelize frontier towns.

Difficulties surround the tent-making strategy: the physical drain of holding a full-time job and also doing missionary
work; restrictions on witnessing by employer or government; lack of follow-up when the missionary leaves; and
isolation from lack of fellowship at a local church.

But tent making has advantages: access to countries
closed to missionaries, such as the Communist block and
Muslim countries; access to those in parallel professions in
the closed nations; avoidance of unnecessary interrogation
by omitting the word *missionary* on the passport applica-
tion; and use of special skills to assist an already established
missionary enterprise. Missiologists estimate that by the year
2000, over 80 percent of the nations will be closed to missionaries. To reach an estimated 5 billion people by then,
future tentmakers should now be preparing and striving for
excellence in their chosen field.

They Were Teachers

Priscilla and Aquila informed Paul how things were at Rome,
capital of the Empire. Strategist Paul foresaw the wisdom of
making Rome a center of evangelism and training. But before heading for Rome, he wanted to start a work in another

important center, namely Ephesus, the hub of Asia Minor and scene of the great temple of Diana. So he devised a plan.

At Ephesus. As a good Jew, Paul tried to make a pilgrimage to Jerusalem to attend the Passover as often as possible. Because he intended to plant a church in Ephesus soon, why not swing around through Ephesus on his way to Jerusalem and leave Priscilla and Aquila there to lay a foundation for the new work? Had he not worked with them for two years? Did he not know their potential? He was well aware of their knowledge of the Scriptures and zeal for outreach. So, "Paul . . . took his leave . . . and sailed . . . and with him Priscilla and Aquila . . . And he came to Ephesus and left them there" (Acts 18:18-19). He would return in a few months to build a strong church.

Paul's confidence was not misplaced. The fruit of his investment in their lives in Corinth soon became evident in Ephesus. Before his return, Priscilla and Aquila became pioneer missionaries at Ephesus, again supporting themselves by their tent-making trade. Warm, hospitable people, they opened their home for study of the Word, and as some responded, for worship. Their home became a church, even though numbers may have been few.

They not only stayed until Paul returned, but they also remained with him for his fruitful ministry there. Paul earned his daily bread during that period, joining them in tent making (Acts 20:34). The length of Paul's stay must have totaled nearly three years, for he taught three months in the synagogue (Acts 19:8), two years in the lecture hall of Tyrannus (v. 10), and then spent additional time in the city (v. 22). Because Paul expressed greetings from Priscilla and Aquila in his letter to the Corinthians, written toward the end of his ministry at Ephesus (1 Cor. 16:19), Priscilla and Aquila must have spent a full three years or more there, opening their home to the young church members as well as assisting Paul.

Instructing an imperfectly informed disciple. While Priscilla and Aquila were ministering alone at Ephesus before Paul's return, "a certain Jew named Apollos, born at Alexandria, an eloquent man, and mighty in the scriptures, came to Ephesus. This man was instructed in the way of the Lord; and being fervent in the spirit, he spake and taught diligently the things of the Lord, knowing only the baptism of John. And he began to speak boldly in the synagogue" (Acts 18:24-26). So Aquila and his wife decided to check him out.

Immediately they detected a defect in his knowledge; however, he taught no blatant error. He denied no fundamental of the faith. His defect was of a different order. He was imperfectly informed. His message was true as far as it went, but it went only as far as the baptism of John. This defect was serious enough to require correction, but because in general he was instructed in the way of the Lord, he needed gentle handling. Priscilla and Aquila knew his limited knowledge could hurt the Christian cause, so they were determined this eloquent teacher should become a fully informed expositor of the Scriptures.

What a wonderful opportunity Apollos afforded these two to display their superior knowledge! They now had a ready-made target for their critical arrows! But such an attack would have wounded this gifted minister and possibly terminated his usefulness.

Using tact. Priscilla and Aquila decided to talk to Apollos. But how would they go about it? They would not treat him like a heretic. They would not talk him down, nor talk down to him, but talk *to* him. Showing no condescension, they took the initiative. Sensing Apollos needed instruction, they created the opportunity to expound "unto him the way of God more perfectly" (Acts 18:26). They would complete his comprehension of the Gospel by filling in the missing facts, providing a detailed, full, thorough account of the redemption story.

Not a word of criticism was uttered in the synagogue. Nothing was said openly which would have embarrassed the church. Showing consummate tact, they invited Apollos to their home one Sabbath. Perhaps their approach was something like this: "We see that you are a stranger in our city. We were glad to hear you speak in the synagogue today. We'd like to invite you to come home with us for dinner." No word was spoken about the sermon on the way home, nor during the meal, which was doubtless a tasty affair.

After dinner all may have retired to the living room where, after some polite conversation, Priscilla and Aquila came to the point. They did not boast of their superior knowledge, nor of their close companionship with Paul, nor of their privileged two-year personal instruction from him in Corinth. They told Apollos that there was another and greater message than John the Baptist had preached. Jesus the Messiah had come. He had died, risen, ascended to heaven, and sent the Holy Spirit. Then Priscilla and Aquila led the young and fiery preacher from verse to verse through the Old Testament Scriptures, even as they had heard Paul do so many times in his synagogue sermons and person-to-person witness. Apollos came to a personal knowledge of sins forgiven through the crucified, risen Christ and experienced the indwelling of the Holy Spirit, given to all believers.

In humility, Apollos learned all he could. Priscilla and Aquila saw that he was a logical choice to send to the infant church they had so recently left at Corinth. His wide grasp of the Old Testament would make him a competent apologist with the Jews, and his oratorical prowess would give him a ready hearing with the Greeks. They were not mistaken in their evaluation. He spoke with such success at Corinth that many people, contrasting his brilliance with Paul's unsophistication, began to create the Apollos party without his approval and against his will. Perhaps this action helped to speed Apollos' exit from Corinth.

Priscilla and Aquila multiplied themselves through Apollos' ministry. Someone said, "If we cannot be great, we can help to make others great." We increase our usefulness and influence by helping others with greater abilities than we possess. The record of Apollos' ministry in Achaia states, "On arriving, he was a great help to those who by grace had believed. For he vigorously refuted the Jews in public debate, proving from the Scriptures that Jesus was the Christ" (Acts 18:27-28, NIV).

They Were Travelers
Bill Fuqua is listed in the Guinness Book of World Records as the champion at doing nothing. He stands so absolutely still in his routines in shopping malls or fun parks that people mistake him for a mannequin. He discovered his talent at age 14 when, for a prank, he stood motionless by a Christmas tree until a woman, touching him, exclaimed, "Oh, I thought it was a real person!"

Priscilla and Aquila were never stationary. They made long, tiring trips. Someone facetiously suggested they were the Howard Johnsons of the tent-making world with a chain of tent-making shops in Rome, Corinth, and Ephesus.

We can trace their itinerary with some degree of completeness over a 16-year period. About A.D. 51 they left Rome because of Emperor Claudius' edict to evict all Jews from the city and arrived in Corinth. After two years in Corinth, they spent three years in Ephesus, up to ten years back in Rome, and then returned to Ephesus again by the time of Paul's second imprisonment, roughly A.D. 67.

Rome. It's likely that Priscilla and Aquila were Christians in those early years before leaving Rome, perhaps through the efforts of some of those "strangers of Rome" who had been present at Pentecost (Acts 2:10). Also, they were likely active in their witness; then came the expulsion edict. On to Corinth.

Corinth. Earlier we saw how Priscilla and Aquila met Paul in Corinth through their mutual occupation, invited him to stay in their home, and helped the apostle in his fruitful church-planting enterprise. They learned from him, and he, in turn, was strengthened by their hospitality, fellowship, support, and encouragement. Realizing their value, Paul took them to Ephesus to start and nourish the work there until he could return from his Jerusalem pilgrimage.

Ephesus. When Paul wrote the Corinthians from Ephesus, he included this greeting, "Aquila and Priscilla greet you warmly in the Lord, and so does the church that meets in their house" (1 Cor. 16:19, NIV). Paul's extensive stay in Ephesus produced a large church which, though branching out to meet in several homes, began in the Priscilla-Aquila residence.

Because the early disciples had no church building, they had to worship in members' homes. How would the early Christians have survived apart from the openness of homes like those of Mary in Jerusalem, Cornelius in Caesarea, Lydia in Philippi, Philemon in Colosse, and Priscilla and Aquila in every city they lived in?

Rome, again. After Emperor Claudius died, Priscilla and Aquila returned to Rome for several years. Paul, at Corinth toward the end of his third missionary journey, wrote a letter to the church at Rome which he wanted to visit after another pilgrimage to Jerusalem. In this epistle he sent this message, "Greet Priscilla and Aquila, my fellow workers in Christ Jesus. They risked their lives for me. Not only I but all the churches of the Gentiles are grateful to them. Greet also the church that meets at their house" (Rom. 16:3-4, NIV).

They were called fellow workers. Paul placed them by his side. They were special people. No list of Paul's friends would be complete without this godly and loyal couple. His former pupils had developed into valuable associates.

Moreover, they risked their lives for Paul, literally laid back their necks for the executioner's ax. Was it during the attack on Paul at Corinth (Acts 18:12), or during the mob scene at Ephesus (Acts 19:23-41) when the couple endangered their lives to save Paul's? Maybe they hid him under a pile of tent cloth. For this act as well as for many other good works, all the churches were most grateful. This couple was well-known and highly honored. One of the oldest catacombs in Rome, *The Coemeteruim Priscilla*, was named in Priscilla's honor. And a church, also in Rome, carries the inscription, "Titulus Aquila and Prisca." (Prisca is the diminutive of Priscilla.)

Ephesus again. The couple might have left Rome to return to Ephesus because of Nero's persecution, or maybe because of a new assignment by Paul. During his final imprisonment, Paul wrote Timothy, pastoring at Ephesus, "Salute Prisca and Aquila" (2 Tim. 4:19).

The nomadic, migratory life of this couple did not make for ease and convenience but reflects their missionary zeal. Today when we move from one city to another, we hire a mover or rent a truck with all losses covered by insurance. Priscilla and Aquila used a beast of burden to carry their few possessions over dusty, dangerous roads. Some of the trip would have been by sea on rat-infested, unsanitary boats, stalked by preying pirates.

Upon their arrival in a city, they would again open their home for the church to meet. Hospitality was their habit. They structured their lives so that others could be reached through their home. They could not have been used so effectively had they not been hospitable to strangers and welcomed the church to meet inside their walls. In every city in which they lived, they became active in Christian work.

They Were a Team
Never mentioned separately, this couple indisputably operated as a husband and wife team. Though they worked harmoniously, of the two, the wife seems to be the more prominent. Some commentators make Paul out to be a woman-hater, but they forget his appreciation for Lois and Eunice of Lystra, and for Syntyche, Euodias, and Lydia of Philippi, to name a few of the women mentioned by name in his Epistles! This supposed hater of women had quite a bevy of female associates. Priscilla must have been a capable and godly worker in her own right for Paul to mention her along with her husband. No other coworker of Paul's ever had his wife's name mentioned together with his name.

More than that, Paul placed Priscilla's name ahead of Aquila's name in four of the six references. This remarkable woman may have excelled her husband. Her name is found more often than his in history and on inscriptions. Some think she was the more profound teacher, the stronger in character, the leader in entertaining, and the earlier and more mature Christian. She was a remarkable woman, able to combine business, home duties, devotional life, and Christian service.

Yet husband and wife functioned as partners, meshing harmoniously in all aspects of life. They believed the same doctrines, exercised similar faith, possessed the same social and spiritual interests, enjoyed the same friends, and showed the same willingness to commit themselves in sacrifice to the cause of Christ. In the truest sense, they were no more two but one.

Any successful marriage needs affinity not only on the

physical level, but also on the intellectual, emotional, social, and above all, spiritual levels. Joining hands and hearts in the Lord's work adds to the success of marriage. Priscilla and Aquila had become one in a special way as they labored together as joint heirs of the grace of God. The marriage of these self-supporting missionaries is a model from the Apostolic Era of the potential for good through the working together of a Christian husband-wife team.

Tradition says that Priscilla and Aquila were beheaded for their faith. In the Roman Catholic church their names are commemorated on July 8th in the history of martyrs. Apparently then, they were also together in death—a team to the end.

10. Apollos, the Orator

After the disastrous hurricane that struck Long Island in November, 1950, one of the residents took a walk along the south shore. *Reader's Digest,* in its February 1951 edition, explains that as this man was viewing the wrecked cottages and sympathizing with the owners, he came upon a scene that showed how a victim's sense of humor had triumphed over calamity. The white front door of an almost totally wrecked house was propped up by a broken chair. On the door this message was printed in black crayon:

I AM AN INSURANCE SALESMAN
I SELL STORM INSURANCE
I DID NOT CARRY STORM INSURANCE ON THIS
COTTAGE
I AM A DOPE

One Sabbath a visiting teacher showed up in the synagogue at Ephesus and charmed the congregation with his eloquence, knowledge of the Scriptures, and fervency. But because he was deficient in his knowledge of Gospel truth, he stood in a place of great danger. His lack of the full truth could lead others astray. He also led himself astray because he needed to receive the Lord Jesus as his own Saviour in order to experience salvation personally. He had not yet taken out eternal insurance.

His Qualifications

Despite his deficiency, Apollos was a man of great competence. The Scripture describes him as: "a certain Jew ... born at Alexandria, an eloquent man, and mighty in the scriptures. ... This man was instructed in the way of the Lord; and being fervent in the spirit, he spake and taught diligently the things of the Lord. ... And he began to speak boldly in the synagogue" (Acts 18:24-26).

He is an Alexandrian. Apollos had been born in Alexandria, founded by Alexander the Great and located in Egypt on the Mediterranean, near the Nile. One of the most celebrated cities of the Empire, the metropolis of Egypt, and the center of commerce and wealth, Alexandria boasted the greatest library of antiquity and a famous university. Repeated dispersions of Jews had filled the Jewish quarter of the city with tens of thousands of industrious, successful expatriates.

As a center of both Greek and Hebrew cultures, the teachings of Plato and Moses met here. While holding on to their traditional faith, the Jews exposed their children to the learning of the city. One of the best known philosophers of that period was Philo, who tried to reconcile Hellenism and Judaism. Other learned professors gave lectures in grammar, rhetoric, astronomy, mathematics, geography, and medicine. Apollos studied in this environment. Because Paul was also trained in the learning of the day, he could appreciate Apollos' high-quality education.

Apollos was eloquent. Moses claimed weakness in speech, so God gave him Aaron as his mouthpiece. (Ex. 4:10-16). Paul was criticized as contemptible of speech (2 Cor. 10:10). But Apollos' severest critics could not charge him with lack of eloquence. Though Moses and Paul were among the most outstanding representatives of Old and New Testaments, neither possessed fluency of tongue to accompany his depth of intellect. But Apollos possessed both keenness of mind and oratorical prowess. A skillful speaker, he could express his opinions with force. He may have been the most articulate and forceful preacher in the early church.

He was mighty in the Scriptures. Apollos had devoted his learning and eloquence to the exposition of the Old Testament, the Bible of his day. He knew how to use the Scriptures to reach men's hearts. A preacher needs to know all possible background material including language, history, scholarship problems, and social conditions, but all of that is of little avail unless he knows the Bible itself. Apparently, Apollos' character backed up his biblical convictions and made him powerful in his presentation.

Great preachers have always known their Bibles well, proving over and over that the Word is living and active and sharper than any double-edged sword (Heb. 4:12). John A. Broadus, who wrote the classic text on homiletics, *A Treatise on the Preparation and Delivery of Sermons,* (Harper & Brothers) chose Apollos for the subject of his last lecture in his New Testament class at Southern Baptist Seminary. He made a stirring appeal to young ministers to be "mighty in the Scriptures."

Apollos was fervent in spirit. Fervent means literally "boiling over" or "burning." He was passionate and enthusiastic. He did not lack the courage of his convictions but spoke boldly in the synagogue. The same adverb *boldly* is used to describe Paul's manner of preaching in the same synagogue a little later (Acts 19:8).

He taught diligently, or accurately. Since an enthusiastic speaker sometimes tends to exaggerate or embellish the facts, we admire Apollos' restrained rhetoric in matters concerning the Lord. He wanted others to know the truth as he knew it. But herein lay his problem. As far as his knowledge went, he was an extremely effective exponent of God's Word; however, his knowledge didn't go far enough. His deficient grasp of truth was dangerous, jeopardizing his own soul, as well as the souls of his hearers.

People today may be heavily involved in church work and be knowledgeable, zealous, and highly qualified, yet lack a critical understanding of the basic New Testament message.

His Deficiency

To illustrate the nature of Apollos' deficiency, Dr. Donald Grey Barnhouse drew a parallel from early American history. Many colonists, living in Virginia in the middle of the eighteenth century, started the long trek across the mountains toward the lure of the West. Some, forced to stop because of illness, breakdown of a wagon axle, or some other unforeseen difficulty, settled in the sheltered valleys of the mountains of what is today eastern Tennessee or Kentucky. Their farewell greeting to their friends in Virginia in 1770 had been, "God Save The King."

Cut off from the world completely, 15 years went by before they saw any traveler. Imagine the excitement when the noise of an arriving caravan ran through the valley. After making sure this was a friendly group, they engaged in animated conversation. After a while one of the settlers got around to asking, "And who is King now? Is it still George the Third?"

The answer came immediately, "There is no King now!

We've had a revolution and a long war! The colonies won! Now we are a republic, and George Washington is our President!"

The settlers thought a moment and replied, "Imagine that! For 15 years we've thought of ourselves as loyal subjects of the King, and now we discover that we are Americans, citizens of our own republic. God bless the President!" (*Epistle to the Romans,* Booklet 31, Evangelical Foundation, p. 1571)

Apollos had been caught in the transitory stage between John's baptism and Pentecost, just as the settlers in Kentucky had lived through the transition period from King George III to President George Washington without a realization of the change. At some point Apollos had made contact with some disciples of John the Baptist. Perhaps he had received baptism at their hands. He may also have learned something about the life and teachings of the Lord Jesus without understanding His death, resurrection, ascension, and sending of the Holy Spirit on the Day of Pentecost to begin the church.

Though eloquently presented, Apollos' message sounded as if John the Baptist were still preaching and baptizing 25 years later. John's teachings and warnings were thundered by Apollos with all the Baptist's fervor but with a much more polished and perfected style. After hearing Apollos preach, Priscilla and Aquila realized with increasing distress that this gifted orator and Bible student was proclaiming a pre-Crucifixion, pre-Resurrection, and pre-Pentecost Gospel.

Apollos wasn't the first church worker who failed to go beyond the life of Jesus in his preaching but instead emphasized His social justice and ethical teachings. Such people preach Jesus as example but never proclaim Him as Saviour. The true Gospel says we need Him as Saviour first; then He gives us the strength to follow His example.

Apollos possessed incomplete knowledge, not erroneous data. In no way was he a heretic. How wonderful if inadequately informed workers today could receive the diplomatic, courteous, and reconciliatory treatment accorded Apollos.

His Enlightenment

Priscilla and Aquila felt ambivalent about this remarkable preacher. How gifted and forceful, yet he was not fully informed. But what to do about it?

It's easy to imagine what most of us would do. First, we would fidget in our seats. Then, we would shift and squirm. Next, we would look at the clock to see how many more minutes of agony we had to endure. Acting subconsciously, we might cover our eyes with our hands, or bow our heads in embarrassment. We might glance around at other parishioners to see how they were taking it and smile sadly and knowingly. At the door we might ask others, "How did you like him?" and without waiting for a reply, comment, "Poor man. He's ignorant of the Gospel basics." Before long the criticism would have reached Apollos' ears, driving him out of the synagogue, perhaps closing the door to all future service.

We can be sure Priscilla and Aquila did not discuss the sermon at the church door or at home in front of their children. If asked by son or daughter about the sermon, the answer would have been, "Apollos comes from Alexandria, the great center of learning. He put a lot of work into that sermon. He had some good lessons for us to learn." But later when the children were asleep, the parents would be quite frank with each other. They recognized a diamond in the rough in need of polishing, so they hit upon a plan of action. They would invite him home for a meal and tactfully fill in the blanks in his message.

Soul-winning is just that—not scolding, not overpowering, not trickery, but winsomeness. When spiritual surgery is needed, the knife must be bathed in love and rendered sterile by the Holy Spirit. No surgeon rushes into the operating room and lashes out at a patient with his scalpel. Apollos has a lot going for him and needed to be handled with care and tact.

In preparation for the spiritual surgery, Priscilla and Aquila likely served Apollos dinner. Afterwards in the parlor, the couple gently brought the conversation around to the things of God. Not only had the One proclaimed by John the Baptist appeared on the scene, they explained, but He had died as the Lamb to take away sin. Then He rose triumphantly from the grave, ascended to the Father's right hand, and sent the Holy Spirit who baptized all believers (from the Day of Pentecost on) into the body of Christ, which is the church.

His Reaction

As he learned the things that had occurred after John's ministry, Apollos' eyes must have moistened, hearing of the sufferings of the Lord Jesus and of His exaltation to the Father's right hand from which He had sent the Spirit. He readily saw how all this information fit with what he had already been taught in Alexandria, fulfilling the Old Testament prophecies. He now saw the complete picture: "the New Testament in the Old contained, and the Old Testament by the New explained."

Some have wondered who is to be more admired: Priscilla and Aquila for their superior wisdom, bravery, and tact, or Apollos for his humility, docility, and teachability. Imagine this learned Alexandrian scholar, crowd-swaying synagogue orator, and mighty student of the Scriptures, being confronted by an untrained commoner couple in the congregation who earned their living by making tents out of goat skins.

What irony that this educated rhetorician was being taken to task and told how to preach by this unschooled couple, one of whom was a woman, no less.

But Apollos saw what a treasure he had in this couple. In reality he regarded them as his superiors in the truth of the Gospel and displayed deep appreciation for the new light which had now been shed on his deficient understanding. Gladly would he surrender all his university diplomas, oratorical trophies, and attentive audiences to sit at the feet of this lowly couple who could teach him more and more about Jesus.

This wasn't the first time that the so-called wise had been set straight by the simple, or as Jesus put it: spiritual truth hidden from "the wise and prudent, and revealed . . . unto babes" (Matt. 11:25). John Bunyan in *Grace Abounding* tells how he was greatly helped by overhearing women of poor station conversing about the things of God. He reported how one day in the providence of God, working in the streets of Bedford, he saw:

> three or four poor women sitting at a door in the sun, and talking about the things of God; and being now willing to hear their discourse, I drew near to hear what they said, for I was now a brisk talker myself in the matter of religion. But I may say, I heard, but I understood not; for they were far above, out of my reach. Their talk was about a new birth, the work of God in their hearts, also how they were convinced of their miserable state by nature. They talked how God had visited their souls with His love in the Lord Jesus, and with what words and promises they had been refreshed, comforted, and supported against the temptations of the devil. And, methought, they spoke as if joy did make them speak; they spoke with such pleasantness of Scripture language, and

with such an appearance of grace in all they said, that they were to me, as if they had found a new world, as if they were people that dwelt alone, and were not to be reckoned among their neighbors. Therefore I should often make it my business to be going again and again into the company of these poor people, for I could not stay away. And presently I found two things within me at which I did sometimes marvel; the one was a very great softness and tenderness of heart; and the other was a great bending of my mind to a continual meditating on them (Alexander Whyte, *Bible Characters, Stephen to Timothy,* Revell, pp. 271-272).

Bunyan attributed his conversion to the godly conversation of these lowly peasants.

The heart of Apollos, already warmed by kind hospitality and now touched by the Spirit of God, was ripe for an intelligent acceptance of Jesus Christ as his personal Savior. Dr. Ayer pictures it thus:

Down on their knees they go, Aquila and Priscilla with their arms about the young preacher, the tears coursing down their faces, asking God to have the Lord Jesus come into his heart by the Spirit, to give him a conscious knowledge of sin forgiven through the death and resurrection of the Lord Jesus Christ; to send him forth in a mighty ministry of the Gospel. When they arose from their knees a new light was shining in the face of Apollos. He had been born again. The resurrected Christ was dwelling in his heart" (*Seven Saved Sinners,* Zondervan, p. 123).

Many have had Apollos' experience. Once a young lady came to her pastor with a heavy heart, declaring she did not know Jesus as her Saviour, though she was a good church member. Moreover, she had taught a Sunday School class with seeming success, but she sobbed, "I've never found Jesus, and I want to find Him." That very day she settled the matter.

His Usefulness
Now properly instructed in the Gospel, what a power for the Lord's work he became.

He made an impact at Corinth. The record says, "When [Apollos] was disposed to pass into Achaia, the brethren wrote, exhorting the disciples to receive him" (Acts 18:27). The NIV states that "Apollos wanted to go to Achaia." What made him want to go? The Bezan text (the Latin translation of Theodore Beza, an associate of Calvin's at Geneva, which markedly influenced the translators of the *King James* Bible) has this variation: "And there were certain Corinthians sojourning in Ephesus, and when they heard [Apollos] they besought him to cross over into their country. And when he had consented, the Ephesians wrote to the disciples in Corinth that they should receive the man." Apollos seemed just the type of teacher to suit the situation at Corinth. Priscilla and Aquila, who understood the Corinthian scene well, concurred in the choice of this pulpit committee. Supplied with a letter of recommendation, Apollos headed for Corinth.

He soon justified their endorsement. He became a great help to the new believers there. In addition, he was able to succeed where Paul didn't seem to have too much success. "He vigorously refuted the Jews in public debate, proving from the Scriptures that Jesus was the Christ" (Acts 18:27-28, NIV). We recall that the Jews in Corinth had blasphemed Paul and dragged him before Gallio for teaching this very doctrine (Acts 18:6, 12-17). More of an apologist and teacher than an evangelist, Apollos built on what Paul had sown

141

(1 Cor. 3:6, 11). Paul started the church; Apollos nourished and developed it. The parched, drooping converts at Corinth flourished again under Apollos' ministry.

The spirit of dissension among believers is not his fault. Apollos' philosophical approach and polished style charmed the fickle Corinthians. Church members began to compare the relative merits of Paul and Apollos. Then someone introduced the name of Peter, who may have made a brief visit there. Folks began to line up behind one of these three until someone very spiritually declared, "I follow Christ."

Sad to say, churches have been divided over one leader or another over and over again throughout history. I have in my files a news story about a church in Pennsylvania where police were called in to maintain order between two factions, one of which met upstairs, led by a pastor who was voted out but refused to leave. The other faction convened downstairs, led by a returned missionary at the invitation of the official leaders of the congregation.

In no way did the spirit of dissension at Corinth develop because of any deliberate act on the part of Apollos. Rather, it resulted from a fault common to those who line up behind human leaders; they fail to see that God uses all types of servants in His work.

He leaves Corinth. Not until after Apollos left Corinth did the four divisions develop fully. Perhaps a premonition of trouble hastened his departure. Apollos would never have been a party to the spirit which controlled the Apollos party. It was a visit from the household of Chloe to Paul at Ephesus that brought news of the schisms at Corinth (1 Cor. 1:11-12). In no way did Paul reproach Apollos for any part in causing the problem. Rather, his comments in 1 Corinthians on the divisions show him to be on the best of terms with Apollos. Doubtless, Paul and Apollos discussed the tragic situation before Paul wrote his reply.

Paul pointed out to the Corinthians the folly of making heroes out of humans who are but servants of God. If they would recognize these leaders as members of the same team, they would not foolishly pit personalities against each other. Paul, Apollos, and Peter were instruments in God's hands, recipients of God's gifts, performing services that were ineffective apart from divine empowerment. Each one could do only a part of God's work. Though Paul "planted" and Apollos "watered" the seed of God's Word, only God gave the increase (1 Cor. 3:6). Why exalt fallible men, all of whom must face the judgment of their Master some day? Paul suggested that the Corinthians, by frivolously evaluating God's servants, were usurping a prerogative of God.

Apollos and Paul could easily have envied each other, but they readily recognized they were co-workers in the Lord's service, each doing his task in his own way, and rejoicing in each other's success. Paul had such confidence in Apollos that he urged him to accompany some brethren going to Corinth (1 Cor. 16:12). Paul believed nothing better could happen than to have Apollos visit Corinth and warn the brethren against idolizing human leaders. But Apollos wisely stayed away from Corinth. He had not started the trouble, and did not wish to fan the flame by showing up in person then. But he would not close the door to a future visit at an opportune time (1 Cor. 16:12).

Apollos and Paul continued to be the best of friends. The last we hear of Apollos is in Paul's epistle to Titus. Apollos is on a trip through Crete with lawyer Zenas, probably the bearers of this letter written after Paul's first Roman imprisonment. Titus is to furnish help to Apollos and Zenas on their missionary journey (Titus 3:13).

So Apollos is still at it, eloquent, fervent, and even mightier in the Scriptures.

11. Philip, the Evangelist

A visitor, leaning on a fence, was watching an old farmer plowing with a mule which didn't seem to know which way to go. The visitor commented, "I hope you don't think I'm telling you how to run your business, but you could save yourself a lot of time and energy if you'd say 'Giddyap' and 'Whoa' to your mule, instead of just pulling and tugging on those reins."

The farmer, drawing a hankie from his pocket and wiping his forehead, answered, "You're right. But this animal stepped on my toe five years ago, and I haven't spoken to him since."

Because a grudge is always tougher on the one who holds it, how wise of Philip not to nurse an unforgiving spirit toward Paul because of the persecutor's role in the stoning of Stephen. Probably no one in the early church was closer to Stephen than Philip, a fellow deacon.

Philip must have been deeply mystified when God snuffed out the life of this brilliant apologist and friend. Philip's pain dug deep. When rumor came of Paul's conversion, Philip, like the other believers, thought it a ruse to infiltrate the ranks of the saints in order to persecute them. But when Paul's transformation proved a reality, Philip began to see some semblance of reason in the tragedy of Stephen's death. Recalling how the dying Stephen had prayed for the Lord to forgive his persecutors, including Paul, Philip too was able to forgive. Moreover, as Paul seemed to take on Stephen's mantle as a master apologist, even surpassing the martyr in usefulness, Philip saw how all things did indeed work together for good. He understood how the Lord had used Stephen's stoning. Any bitterness against Paul faded. Philip held no grudge against this old enemy of the church.

Philip, the Deacon

The New Testament calls Philip "the evangelist, one of the Seven" (Acts 21:8, NIV). A collective noun like *the Twelve* which refers to Jesus' disciples, *the Seven* relates to the deacons chosen by the early church to assist the Twelve in the daily distribution of alms in the form of money or food.

Traditionally, the Seven have been called deacons, though that word is not used in Acts. Two of the Seven achieved special mention: Stephen, the apologist-martyr and Philip, the evangelist (Acts 6:1-7). Though we know nothing beyond the names of the other five, Stephen and Philip not only performed their ministry of mercy with the poor, but they also spearheaded aggressive evangelism.

We learn something about Philip by noting the four qualifications for becoming a deacon: "men from among you," "of good report," "full of the Spirit," and "full of wisdom" (Acts 6:3). Here are qualifications not for preachers, but for church officers.

1. Christian workers should be chosen from among the believers. No one should be brought to any board who is not a professing Christian.

2. Christian workers should possess a good reputation. Persons of recognized character should be chosen to carry out the business of the church.

3. Christian workers should be godly people, full of the Spirit. This does not mean abandoning earthly interests, but rather placing such interests under the lordship of Christ.

4. Christian workers should also be full of wisdom, dominated by sanctified common sense.

Philip, along with the other members of the Seven, exercised divinely given tact and wisdom in the administration of daily resources to the satisfaction of all parties concerned. It seems that Philip had many gifts. Not only did he have the gift of wisdom, but he also must have possessed the gift of showing mercy as he helped to distribute resources to alleviate the burdens of those early saints.

Aristides, a Christian philosopher, in presenting a defense of the Christian faith to Roman Emperor Hadrian around A.D. 133, described the early church thus, "They love one another, they never fail to help widows, they save orphans from those who would hurt them. If they have something they give freely to the man who has nothing. If they see a stranger they take him home, and are as happy as though he were a real brother" (Charles Colson, *Presenting Belief in an Age of Unbelief,* Victor, p. 35).

Philip, the Evangelist

Philip is called the evangelist, the only one so described in the New Testament (Acts 21:8). The word, however, is used on two other occasions. Timothy is urged to "do the work of an evangelist (2 Tim. 4:5). To build up His church, God gifted people as apostles, prophets, pastors, teachers, and evangelists (Eph. 4:11).

The word *evangelist* comes from two words which mean "good" and "announce." The evangelist is a proclaimer of

Good News, a specially gifted person endowed by the ascended Lord to build the church numerically. He possesses a clear grasp of the Gospel, a deep passion to herald it, an abiding confidence that God will cause hearers to respond, and the satisfying joy of seeing converts.

Philip the evangelist stands at the forefront of all evangelists, not only because he is the first one so named, but also because of his evangelistic ministry recorded in Acts. Though Stephen and Philip were not ordained as ministers of the Word, these two godly and gifted men could not be limited to the serving of tables. The presence of such competent men among the Seven is a tribute to the discernment of that early congregation as well as to the rich pool of talent in the Apostolic Church. Perhaps Paul had Stephen and Philip in mind when he wrote, "For they that have used the office of a deacon well purchase to themselves a good degree, and great boldness in the faith which is in Christ Jesus" (1 Tim. 3:13). Faithful completion of their deacon responsibilities led to a clear and courageous witness in their preaching. An entire chapter is devoted to the aggressive ministry of each one. Acts 7 (and Acts 6:9-15) relates Stephen's apology for the Christian faith before the Sanhedrin while Acts 8 covers Philip's evangelistic efforts, first a successful citywide crusade in Samaria, then a one-to-one soul-winning effort in the Gaza desert.

In the city of Samaria. Philip is the first missionary on record who evangelized an alien race. When persecution scattered the believers, Samaria seemed an unlikely target of evangelism. Were not the Samaritans, an amalgamation of northern Jews and Assyrian heathen with their own temple and faulty rituals, despised by the Jews? The Gospels tell us how the Jews had no dealings with the Samaritans.

Yet Jesus acted much differently toward these half-breed people. At the well of Samaria, He deliberately struck up a conversation with a woman of bad repute who had been married five times. He led her to trust in Him as the Messiah, then unleashed her as a missionary to her fellow Samaritans (John 4:1-42). In His teaching, as a model of kindness, Jesus used the example of a "good Samaritan," the last person in the world to whom a Jew would have attributed such a virtue (Luke 10:30-37). He also noted that, of ten lepers whom He miraculously healed, the only one to return to say thanks was a Samaritan (Luke 17:12-19). Finally, Jesus' last command expressly charged His followers to be witnesses in Samaria (Acts 1:8). All these episodes were not lost on Philip, though as a Hellenist, he probably had less trouble in transcending racial bias.

Philip, the evangelist, "went down to the city of Samaria, and preached Christ unto them" (Acts 8:5). The crowds paid close attention to his message. Hanging on his every word, they watched as unclean spirits were cast out, and paralytics and lame people walked. Great joy enveloped the city. Remarkably, Philip was used to break the spell of a sorcerer who through trickery had hoodwinked the people into thinking of him as "the great power of God" (Acts 8:10). Though the sorcerer's conversion later appeared less than genuine, he did lose his hold on the masses.

When the apostles in Jerusalem heard that Samaria had received the Gospel, they immediately sent Peter and John to investigate this new advance of Gospel preaching, even as they later would examine the reports of Gentile believers in Cornelius' household and at Antioch. Would Philip resent apostolic intrusion into his fruitful ministry at Samaria? To his credit he was in no way threatened but rather delighted at the visit by Peter and John who encouraged him by praying that the Samaritan believers might receive the Holy Ghost.

The noble conduct of Peter and John is also worthy of

note. As apostles and superiors, wouldn't they be tempted to begrudge the successful labors of Philip, merely one of the Seven and a subordinate? To their credit they in no way debunked the victories of Philip in Samaria, even as they also had not envied the apologetic capability of Stephen at Jerusalem. They didn't remind Philip that his proper place was serving tables, not preaching, nor did they judge all that had happened as mere Samaritan emotion. Their worthy behavior reflected their apostolic office. Pitching right in to help nurture the converts, they "testified and preached the word of the Lord." On their return trip, motivated by Philip's success, they "preached the Gospel in many villages of the Samaritans" (Acts 8:25). More than likely, the influence of the Samaritan woman, won by Jesus at the well a few years earlier, helped pave the way for the success of this Samaritan crusade.

In the Gaza Desert. Recently, Alex Leonovich, executive secretary of the Slavic Missionary Service, and his wife were invited by the evangelical Christians of Russia to visit the Soviet Union and preach in the evangelical churches. Driving a taxi to their hotel, their handsome, young cabdriver, amazed that these tourists from America spoke Russian, asked how they learned the language. When Leonovich told him of their Russian roots, the driver asked his occupation. Telling of his radio broadcasts aimed at proclaiming the message of peace through the Prince of Peace, he noticed the driver turn pale and quiet. Evidently in a state of minor shock, the driver told how his mother, a Christian, had suffered a paralyzing stroke and for 12 bedridden years her only joy was to listen on her shortwave radio to the Russian programs aired over Trans World Radio-Monte Carlo. "Not only were the messages a source of strength to her," said the cabdriver, "but I listened too. No wonder your voice was familiar to me. I am shocked now when I realize you are the one I used to hear preach the Word of God on the air."

The young driver continued, "Two years ago my mother died. As I stood by her bedside, she said she was praying that someone might come from a far country and tell me the way of salvation in more detail. As I listen now to you, it's not your voice I'm hearing, but my mother's last words to me."

The cabdriver arranged for a meeting with Leonovich the next afternoon in a park away from the crowds at the hotel. There, for more than an hour, Leonovich and the driver discussed spiritual matters. The cabdriver accepted Christ. The two men met as strangers but parted brothers in the faith, though probably never to meet again here on earth. The Lord had arranged the meeting ("Met as Strangers, Parted as Brothers," *Trans World Radio,* Winter 1986, pp. 10-11).

Though differing in details, the Lord had set up a similar rendezvous between Philip, the evangelist, and an Ethiopian seeker whose heart had been prepared through the reading of the Word. Philip must have wondered when a messenger from the Lord told him to leave Samaria, scene of mass conversions, and go down to the Gaza desert. Obediently, Philip arose and went. The story of Philip's one-on-one soul-winning episode is recorded in Acts 8:26-40.

As he walked along the desert highway, puzzled as to why the Lord had led him here, Philip spotted a well-to-do caravan coming his way. In the center of the caravan was a high Ethiopian official, the treasurer for Queen Candace. This government official was returning, not from a political assignment, but from a religious pilgrimage to Jerusalem, no small journey of over 1,200 miles. Somehow he had acquired a copy of the Scriptures and was reading aloud.

Told by the Spirit to approach this chariot, Philip ran toward the Ethiopian and heard him reading from Isaiah 53.

When Philip asked if he understood what he was reading, the Ethiopian replied, "Come up, sit beside me, and explain it to me." He ordered his driver to stop the chariot, so Philip could climb in. Pointing to the Isaiah passage, the Ethiopian asked, "Is Isaiah speaking of himself, or of someone else?" Because Isaiah 53 gives such graphic pictures of the suffering and victory of Christ, it was easy for Philip to begin at this passage of Scripture and preach to him Jesus as the Man of sorrows, despised and rejected of men. He explained how Jesus was wounded for our transgressions, numbered with the transgressors, and put to death on the cross. He went on to explain how Jesus rose from the dead and forgives all who repent and believe in Him. Philip did not preach Jesus as a mere prophet, great thinker, saintly character, or social reformer, but rather as the suffering, crucified, living Saviour.

The Ethiopian opened his heart to the Lord Jesus. Philip had evidently spoken of baptism in his presentation of the Gospel. Had not Jesus' Great Commission included making disciples and also baptizing them? As the chariot rolled along the desert road, it came to a body of water. The Ethiopian said, "Look, here is water. Why shouldn't I be baptized?" (Acts 8:36, NIV) After the new convert's confession of faith, both went down into the water for the baptismal service; then they parted.

In both the public city witness and in the private desert evangelism, the message was the same. Philip preached Jesus Christ. In both instances conversion was followed by baptism (Acts 8:12, 38). In both settings joy abounded: the city had great joy (Acts 8:8), and the Ethiopian went on his way rejoicing (Acts 8:39).

In the Towns from Azotus to Caesarea. Caught away by the Spirit, Philip was found at Azotus, also known as the Philistine city of Ashod. He passed through all the towns from Azotus to Caesarea, probably through Ekron, Joppa, Appolonia, and the plain of Sharon. But as he traveled that route, he also preached the Gospel, always the evangelist.

Philip was a lay person, not ordained, not one of the Twelve. But you don't have to be a pastor or even an evangelist to have the gift of evangelism. Dr. Peter Wagner of Fuller Seminary said:

> The average Christian church can realistically expect that approximately 10 percent of its active adult members will have been given the gift of evangelism. If God blesses a church by giving the gift of evangelism to more than 10 percent of its members, it is in wonderful shape for growth. (*Your Spiritual Gifts Can Help Your Church Grow,* Regal, p. 177)

Even those without the gift can have a share in winning the lost.

Near the turn of this century a salesman named Rigby traveled frequently to Edinburgh on business. When there over a Sunday, he would invariably go to hear Alexander Whyte preach. He would also invite fellow businessmen to accompany him to the services of this large church. One Sunday morning a fellow traveler reluctantly agreed to go. He was so impressed by Whyte's sermon that he returned with Rigby to the evening service where, sitting quietly in his seat, he received Christ as his Saviour. The next morning as he walked by the pastor's study, Rigby felt constrained to stop and inform him how his friend had been converted through the message. When Whyte heard the caller's name was Rigby, he excitedly exclaimed, "You're the man I've wanted to meet for years." Pulling from his desk a bundle of letters, he read Rigby a few excerpts, all relating how lives were changed, and all mentioning a man named Rigby as the one who brought them to hear the Gospel ("A Faithful Witness," *Our Daily Bread,* May 15, 1986).

Philip, the Host
Would you invite the murderer of your close friend into your home for a stay of several days? Philip did.

Twenty years go by before we hear of Philip again. Acts 8 ends with Philip journeying through the towns from Azotus to Caesarea where, apparently, he settled down. The next time we meet Philip he is living at Caesarea. At this time Paul is on his final visit to Jerusalem; with him are eight delegates commissioned to take an offering from the Gentile churches to the poor saints in Jerusalem. They stopped at Caesarea, writes Luke, one of the delegates, and "we entered into the house of Philip the evangelist, which was one of the seven; and abode with him" (Acts 21:8). Philip's home must have been somewhat spacious to accommodate these guests for "many days" (v. 10).

Often the faithful exercise of a gift in one area leads to the discovery and development of a gift in another area. Philip was a man of many gifts. Because he possessed the gift of wisdom, he was chosen as a deacon. Fulfilling the duties of a deacon, he exhibited the gift of showing mercy. His title, the evangelist, was given because of his gift of evangelism. Now he displays the gift of hospitality.

Paul once spent 15 days with Peter (Gal. 1:18). What a glorious exchange of conversation they must have had. Now Paul spent a couple of weeks with Philip. What did they talk about? Philip probably told of the election of the Seven, and how at the time of persecution (tactfully omitting specific reference to Paul's part in it) he went down to Samaria to preach, and also how he led the Ethiopian to Christ.

Then Paul probably told of his early years at Tarsus and of sitting at the feet of Gamaliel. Then with shame he told how he held the clothes of those who stoned Stephen, how he heard Stephen pray for those who stoned him, and how he was gloriously converted on the Damascus road. Doubtless, he told Philip something of his three missionary journeys, and that he would yet suffer many things but it would be worth it all. What moving dialogues they must have had as they reminisced. Long ago Philip had forgiven Paul for the stoning of his fellow deacon. Their fellowship now must be a foretaste of the coming communion of saints in heaven.

In January 1981, rebels shot Chet Bitterman, a Wycliffe missionary, and left his body in a hijacked bus. In April 1982, as a token of international good will, the churches and civic groups of Lancaster County, Pennsylvania, Bitterman's home, presented an ambulance to the Colombia State of Meta where he had been martyred. Chester and Mary Bitterman, parents of the slain linguist in whose honor the ambulance was donated, traveled to Colombia for the presentation. At the ceremony his mother explained, "The reason we're able to do this is because God has taken the hatred from our hearts" (Steve Estes, "Called to Die," *Wycliffe Bible Translators,* pp. 253-254).

Philip's hospitality toward Paul shows that God had taken the hatred from his heart also. Later, when Paul was imprisoned at Caesarea for two years, Philip doubtless lightened the Apostle's incarceration by many a refreshing visit. During the same two-year period, Luke would be a frequent and welcome guest in Philip's home as he continued to amass data for his Gospel and the Book of Acts. You can almost hear Luke quizzing Philip and pressing for further details. Philip loved to answer questions related to the Gospel.

Philip, the Father of Four Prophetesses
Philip, long since married, had four unmarried daughters who prophesied (Acts 21:9). The Holy Spirit endowed these

girls with the spiritual gift of prophesying, speaking forth for God. In any discussion of the place of women in church service we must include the fact that these four women, with the Spirit's gift and evident approval, had a ministry of prophecy.

Traditions vary as to what happened to Philip and his daughters when rebellion against Rome broke out in A.D. 65, beginning in their home city of Caesarea. But wherever they went, his daughters doubtless continued to prophesy, and Philip continued to evangelize.

12. Demas, the Defector

Some years ago I led a four-day Bible conference in a church in Toronto, Canada. On the office wall hung the pictures of the church's current pastor and his four predecessors, including the founder, Charles Templeton. The pastor informed me that Templeton, once a popular preacher, had left the ministry and was no longer engaged in Christian ministry, though from time to time he came into the church service there, taking a seat near the back.

Once a halfback for a top Canadian football team, then a well-known sports cartoonist on the *Toronto Globe,* Templeton founded this church and became a popular young evangelist. He was chosen by Youth for Christ to join a team, which included Billy Graham, headed for Europe to get the youth movement rolling there. Later, feeling the need of more education, he enrolled in Princeton Theological Seminary for a three-year course but did not receive a degree because he lacked a B.A. At seminary old doubts, which were finally to drive him from the ministry, began to harass him. But he became secretary for evangelism for the

National Council of Churches, holding major crusades and rivaling Billy Graham in popularity. He was considered a candidate for some prestigious pulpits. Thirty-six young men entered the ministry because of him.

Then in 1957 he gave up the ministry as a result of months of doubt and indecision that struck at the roots of his faith. "I had to decide whether or not I could accept the deity of Jesus Christ. This would be a serious matter for any Christian but for a man who is preaching to others it was essential that I resolve my difficulty. To remain in the church with my doubts still plaguing me would have been dishonest" (John Clare, "Nothing Succeeds Like Charles Templeton," *Maclean's,* Nov. 8, 1958, p. 58).

Templeton became a celebrity on Canadian national television. He wrote several plays for TV and also ran unsuccessfully for Canadian Parliament. On several visits to Canada I have seen him on TV, performing most winsomely. Once I heard him affirm his lack of certainty in the Christian faith. The editor of *The Observer,* published by the United Church of Canada, called his saga a personal tragedy.

Templeton's story makes me think of Demas, a companion and fellow worker of Paul, who one day suddenly forsook Paul who was then in his final incarceration in the dreaded Mamertine prison in Rome. Just as a traitor was among Jesus' Twelve, the defector Demas was among Paul's close friends.

Dr. Clarence E. Macartney in *Bible Epitaphs* imagines the shock Paul must have received one day when a friend visited him at the jail and broke the news about Demas. Perhaps the visitor was Luke who inquired about Paul's health, specifically asking if the medicine brought on an earlier visit was helping. Paul might have replied, "What matters my thorn in the flesh? Before long I shall have a perfect body." After a pause Paul probably asked, "Where's Demas? I sent the others on missions, but I didn't send him on one. I wanted him to be with me to the end. He's not sick is he? Has he had an accident or been arrested by Nero's soldiers?" Then Luke had to tell Paul that Demas had forsaken the apostle. Demas had been seen heading out of the gates of Rome, mumbling something about going back home to Thessalonica. Sadly, Paul shook his head, repeating the words "forsaken me." He might have added, "What power this world has over the souls of men. I thought Demas had conquered, but now the world has won" (Abingdon-Cokesbury, pp. 112-113). Among the last lines written from his dreadful prison, Paul, deeply disappointed, penned the epitaph of this spiritual calamity, "Demas hath forsaken me, having loved this present world, and is departed unto Thessalonica" (2 Tim. 4:10).

Many have followed Demas' steps. I think of a young man with whom, as a teenager, I used to give testimonies in our church's summer Sunday evening services held outdoors in a large Canadian city. A few years later, while serving with the Royal Canadian Air Force, he wrote to tell me that he had thrown the Christian faith overboard. I also recall a promising young man in a youth group, who not only taught a Sunday School class but also became a Sunday School superintendent. While attending a well-known Bible school, he decided he no longer believed the major doctrines of Christianity. Another Christian college graduate became a Christian Science reader, while another Bible school graduate became a bartender.

In the final weeks of his life, Paul looked backward, forward, then around. His backward gaze brought no regrets, "I have fought a good fight." His forward glance gave joyful anticipation, "Henceforth there is laid up for me a crown of righteousness"(2 Tim. 4:7-8). But looking around, he keenly felt the absence of friends. Only Luke was with him. His other associates had scattered on assignments. But Demas—a few candid strokes of the pen speak volumes. The call of the world had crept into Demas' spirit and extinguished his love for spiritual values.

Demas Lost the Companionship of Paul

We do not know how long Demas had been a believer, nor how long he had been a colaborer with Paul. Though not named as one of those who sailed on the shipwrecked voyage to Rome, he was evidently so fond of Paul that he joined him in his first imprisonment at Rome. From his hired house in the empire's capital, Paul wrote four New Testament epistles, in two of which he sent greetings from Demas. He ended the letter to Philemon with a salutation from Epaphras, my fellowprisoner in Christ Jesus; Marcus, Aristarchus, Demas, Lucas, my fellowlaborers" (vv. 23-24). Demas was also among those sending regards to the Colossian Christians: "Luke, the beloved physician, and Demas, greet you" (Col. 4:14). Demas moved in the best of Pauline company and was well-known among the churches of Asia Minor. He had labored with Paul in earlier years, and now had positioned himself to be of service to Paul, the prisoner.

Again, when Paul was detained at Rome a second time in the jailing that would end in his death, Demas was one of his companions. Were it not for that final reference to Demas, we would regard him as a faithful follower of Christ and a true friend of Paul who could be counted on in any crisis. But tragically, at the end he defected.

Because of his defection, Demas lost the intellectual stimulation of being with Paul. Trained at Tarsus and at the feet of the master rabbi Gamaliel, widely traveled, and a man of letters, Paul was a towering, intellectual giant. Education did not come easily in those days. Even though Paul may have had but a few months to live, Demas could have learned profitably, had he remained close to the prison.

Demas also lost the spiritual comradeship of Paul which was a far greater tragedy. Whether free or jailed, Paul moved with the majestic tread of a conqueror because of his faith. Though jailed by Nero and tried by the emperor, Paul still trusted God. The spiritual influence of Paul rubbed off like a benediction on all who entered his orbit. But by turning away, Demas missed the beneficial example of Paul's Christlikeness those final months.

Demas could have walked the last mile with Paul as he went to his execution, strengthening the apostle, and in turn being strengthened by him. He could have witnessed the triumph of that moment when Paul, faithful unto death, was ushered into the presence of Christ through the swing of the executioner's ax. But he missed the depth of kinship that momentous hour would have afforded.

Who knows, had he not deserted Paul, he might have been the recipient of a New Testament epistle like Timothy and Titus were. Or he might have authored a Gospel like two others whose names are associated with Demas' name in Paul's salutations: Mark and Luke.

Demas Rejected a Martyr's Crown

Christians have been persecuted and martyred in every century. Stephen was stoned. James was beheaded. Many have been beaten or suffered for Christ in one way or another. Now Demas had seen Paul imprisoned for his faith. He knew of many believers who had been put to death because they would not deny Christ. Did he see the handwriting on the wall for Paul? Did he begin to fear that he too might share the same fate? Would Nero jail him also? Would he be clothed in animal skins and fed to the lions in the arena? Or covered with pitch and put on fire to light up the way for Nero's chariots? Or did the block, ax, and headsman seem a likely reality?

As the dread of lions, flames, and torture loomed into clear relief, did he begin to feel sorry for himself? Did he feel he was too young to die? Or life to good to give up? Did the old life with all its pleasures flood his memory? Did some sudden temptation thrust itself into his path? Did he yield and feel too ashamed to face Paul? For some reason he failed, preferring comfort and pleasure to suffering and death.

Incidentally, his infidelity would certainly damage the Christian testimony at Rome. Soldiers guarding Paul might have heard Luke whisper the news of Demas' defection. Some would certainly have heard Paul dictate the letter to Timothy in which he mentioned Demas' departure. The word would get around. Perhaps some soldiers, on the verge of accepting the Gospel because they had seen the fortitude of believers in the face of torture, were now turned off.

An authenticated story, going back to midwinter A.D. 320 tells of an edict by a new Roman emperor which declared that civil servants, including the troops, were to lose their appointments if they refused to offer sacrifices on pagan altars before the local deities. The captain of the vaunted Twelfth Legion, an elite group with an unmatched three-century record in waging war, assembled his troops and read out the decree. Then he added. "Men of the Twelfth Legion, you have shown your courage in battle over and over again. I now call on you to demonstrate your loyalty to our imperial Caesar by obedience to his laws. Tomorrow we will sacrifice to the gods."

Later, two soldiers came to the captain's tent, asking permission to speak. They advised him that there were 40 Christians in the legion who would have nothing to do with the proposed sacrifice to local deities.

Angrily the captain replied, "Tell them that if they take part in the sacrifice, they will be eligible for promotion. If they do not, their armor and rank will be taken away from them, and they will be handed over for torture. Tell them to think it over and choose their advantage."

That night in their encampment the 40 Christians read from the Psalms and lifted their voices in Christian hymns. The next morning when they refused to sacrifice to the gods, the captain pronounced their sentence. With arms bound and ropes around their necks, those refusing to sacrifice were to be led to the shore of a nearby frozen lake. Then, at sundown they were to be stripped naked and escorted to the middle of the lake. Because of their excellent record in battle, these Christians were given the privilege of recanting at any time. A heated bathhouse on the shore was available to anyone prepared to renounce his faith in Christ and offer a pagan sacrifice. A bitter wind lashed over the frozen surface as the soldiers were led shivering in the dusk away from the shore. A sentry, posted on the shore to keep the Christians from the heated bathhouse, warmed himself by a bonfire at the edge of the lake.

The sentry could hear the Christians singing from the center of the frozen lake. But near midnight the singing grew feeble. Straining his ears, above the muffled prayers of the Christians the sentry heard an angelic voice announcing, "40 good soldiers for Christ, and 40 martyrs and 40 crowns."

Then a strange thing happened. The angelic song changed to, "39 good soldiers for Christ, and 39 martyrs and 39 crowns." Suddenly the sentry heard the sound of running feet. One of the Christians was heading for shore with its warm bathhouse. Immediately the sentry yanked off his armor and yelled out to the approaching form, "Here, take my clothes, and I'll take your place!" Stripping off his clothes, the sentry ran naked out to the middle of the frozen lake, chanting as he ran, "40 soldiers for Christ, and 40 martyrs, and 40 crowns."

The next morning the captain ordered the victims brought to land. Their frozen bodies were found huddled in a heap in the middle of the lake. Among them was the sentry who, along with the others, had passed into the presence of his Lord whom he had come to love deeply enough to die for Him, even though he had known Him so briefly (taken from "The Forty Martyrs of Sebaste" by Sherwood E. Wirt, in *Decision* Magazine, Dec. 1963; copyright 1963 Billy Graham Evangelistic Association. Used by permission).

Demas, like the defecting soldier, may have lost his crown unless he repented and turned back to serve the Lord, faithful unto death.

Demas Loved This Present World

The term *world* used this way in the Bible doesn't mean the physical creation with all its beauties, for the Bible is full of admiration for the works of nature. Rather, this term refers to unregenerate civilization, the moral order under the domination of the devil, the sinful world system. Worldliness is anything, though seemingly innocent, that would chill our love for God. Worldliness cannot be confined to a series of rules or practices, nor avoided by renunciation of all worldly comforts and pleasure and withdrawal to an isolated monastery.

The venerable Apostle John, probably longer in the service of Christ than any other follower, had seen more than one promising Christian overcome by the world. He warned, "Love not the world, neither the things that are in the world. If any man love the world, the love of the Father is not in him. For all that is in the world, the lust of the flesh, the lust of the eyes, and the pride of life, is not of the Father, but is of the world. And the world passeth away, and the lust thereof: but he that doeth the will of God abideth for ever" (1 John 2:15-17).

The lust of the flesh is sensualism, the illegitimate gratification of our senses through such practices as fornication and gluttony. The lust of the eye involves covetousness, acquisitiveness, greed, and sexual desire. A young seminary student, walking down the street with his professor who was in his 70s, stared at an exceptionally pretty girl coming in their direction. The youth, aware that the professor had caught him staring, remarked, "I'll sure be glad when I'm so old that things like that won't bother me any more." The professor simply replied, "Me too." The pride of life is the feeling of importance and sense of superiority coming from an inflated ego. Thus, worldliness involves motives, values, and attitudes. Let's not be too hard on Demas unless we are sure that deep down we do not value money, sports, clothes, large homes, success, and security more than we value God.

Around A.D. 250 the church at Carthage easily capitulated under the pressure of a militant Roman emperor. An article by Fred Williams, III in *Trinity Journal* lists the most decisive factor in the church's sudden collapse as a preoccupation with the world. The church's bishop, Cyprian, wrote a treatise on the subject, *On the Lapsed,* in which he says the church failed because of an inordinate interest in money and personal vanity which made it totally unprepared to face the rigors of persecution ("Persecution: a Lesson from the Early Church," Spring 1977, pp. 8-10).

The spirit of worldliness can so easily creep into a believer's life today. Chuck Colson tells how he was once chiding the president of one of the TV networks for not putting on more wholesome family programming like *Chariots of Fire.* Then the TV executive explained that his network had run

Chariots of Fire as its Sunday Night Movie some months before. The same night rival networks ran *On Golden Pond* and *My Mother's Secret Life,* a soap opera about a mother hiding her past as a prostitute. These two programs attracted over 52 percent of the viewing audience, while *Chariots of Fire* attracted only 11 percent of the viewing audience. Of the 65 shows rated that week, *Dallas* was number 1 while *Chariots of Fire* was number 57. The TV executive smugly asked, "So where, Mr. Colson, are your 50 million Christians?" Colson had no answer. Maybe you do (Charles Colson, *Presenting Belief in an Age of Unbelief,* Victor, pp. 17-18).

Demas May Have Lost His Immortal Soul

Paul never said specifically that Demas forsook the Lord. It was Paul he deserted. As Paul writes of Demas' desertion, he thinks of Mark, who years before, on Paul's first missionary journey, had also left him and Barnabas to go back home. Mark had long since returned to the Lord's service. In fact, Paul asks Timothy to bring Mark along because he can be helpful to the apostle (2 Tim. 4:11). If through God's grace Mark had returned, perhaps Demas would too. We can hope this was the story of Demas. Through the years many saints have backslid for a while, then returned to the Lord to serve Him with great zeal to the end of their days.

Possibly Demas never returned. John did write that if any man loved the world, he did not have the love the Father in him (1 John 2:15). Four verses later John wrote, "They went out from us, but they did not really belong to us. For if they had belonged to us, they would have remained with us; but their going showed that none of them belonged to us" (1 John 2:19, NIV). If Demas never did return to the Lord, it might show that he was never a genuine believer. Tragically, in that case, despite his association with Paul and his team, his immortal soul would have been lost.

If he were a real believer, but failed in his dedication, he would have lost a full reward. God must be his final judge.

A Christian, faithful to Christ through all his life and into his retirement years, testified he had been influenced by a legend related by an aged minister. The legend describes an angel talking to an old Christian worker. The angel reached into an inner vault and brought out a crown of incomparable beauty, blazing with countless diamonds. "This was the crown I designed for you when you were a youth, but you refused as a young man to surrender your life completely to the Lord, and the crown is gone."

The angel returned to the vault and came out with another crown, still beautiful, but with fewer jewels. "This was the crown I designed in your mid-life, but you gave that part of your life over to worldly pursuits, and it is gone."

Once more the angel returned to the vault. This time he came back with a simple, plain circlet, without any diamonds. "Here," said the celestial visitor, "is the crown for your old age. This is yours for all eternity."